Any book that begins 'Let's be honest: the ascension of Jesus is weird' gets my attention!

My friends Jonny Woodrow and Tim Chester are excited that Jesus Christ has ascended into heaven and you owe it to yourself to find out why.

Why did it fill the disciples who witnessed it with praise and worship for Jesus, and why should it do the same for us? Why does the ascension explain what is going on in heaven? How is Jesus ruling over the world that so often seems hostile to him? How does the ascension establish the age of mission for the church? And what does it mean that Jesus is our man enthroned in heaven, there on our behalf, securing our salvation?

The writers show us the Bible's answers to these questions and many more. If you have ever wondered why the ascension is critical to being a disciple of Jesus or why it wasn't just a bad strategy by God that removed the main evidence for Christianity, you will find plenty of help here.

Marcus Honeysett
Director of Living Leadership and author of *Finding Joy*, Kent, England

During my many years as a Christian, I can recall hearing only one sermon on the Ascension of Christ. With the publication of Chester and Woodrow's *The Ascension: Humanity in the Presence of God*, I'm grateful to be able to point others to an accessible and inspiring study of this central Christian doctrine. In reading this book, Christians will find their minds sharpened and hearts warmed. Delightfully, the book ends with an Ascension hymn. Theology leads to doxology.

Robert L. Plummer,
Associate Professor of New Testament Interpretation,
The Southern Baptist Theological Seminary, Louisville, Kentucky

Countless books have been written about the meaning of Christ's entrance into the world, but comparatively few about His exit. Yet the implications of the Ascension are in many ways as staggering as those of the Incarnation. Who can say which is more wonderful – that God should descend to earth or that man should rise to heaven?

In this short book, the authors explore the climactic event of Jesus' earthly life and unlock its vital and much-neglected significance. And they do so not in abstract theological terms but in a lively, plain and accessible manner that is biblically rooted throughout.

Sceptics, young believers and longstanding Christians alike will be intrigued and challenged in turn as they come to realise the immense – and immensely practical – consequences of the Ascension. Glorious and unexpected truths are here constantly laid bare for our wonder and our joy.

Jonathan Stephen
Principal,
Wales Evangelical School of Theology (WEST), Bridgend, Wales

Tim Chester and Jonny Woodrow pull back the curtains of the true temple to disclose the glories of the on-going work of the Savior on our behalf. They powerfully reveal the Ascension as fulfillment of what all of Redemptive History foreshadows— that the Lord's own will enter his presence only through the work of the One who can go up into the very clouds of God Almighty. Along the way the seasoned churchmen teach us how to read the two Testaments with great Biblical-theological insight. Meditation upon this exposition of Christ's "going up" will strengthen all aspects of our private and corporate worship, prayer, evangelism, of public kingdom living and of gospel preaching. Chester and Woodrow have given us a gift that will lift our eyes from this temporal horizon to the steppes of eternal joys of our High Priest in heaven.

Eric C. Redmond
Executive Pastoral Assistant and Bible Professor in Residence
New Canaan Baptist Church, Washington, DC
Council Member, *The Gospel Coalition*

The Ascension

Humanity in the Presence of God

TIM CHESTER

AND

JONNY WOODROW

Unless otherwise indicated, all Scripture quotations are taken from the *The Holy Bible New International Version®*, NIV® Copyright © 1973, 1978, 1984, 2011 by Biblica, Inc.™ Used by permission. All rights reserved worldwide.

Scripture quotations marked NASB are taken from the *New American Standard Bible®*, Copyright © 1960, 1962, 1963, 1968, 1971, 1972, 1973, 1975, 1977, 1995 by The Lockman Foundation. Used by Permission. (www.Lockman.org)

Tim Chester is Associate Director of the Porterbrook Seminary, pastor of The Crowded House in Sheffield, and author of over 20 books. He is married with two daughters.

Jonny Woodrow is the European Director of the Porterbrook Network and pastor of The Crowded House in Loughborough. He is married with four children.

Copyright © Tim Chester and Jonny Woodrow 2013
paperback ISBN 978-1-78191-144-0
epub ISBN 978-1-78191-210-2
Mobi ISBN 978-1-78191-212-6

10 9 8 7 6 5 4 3 2 1

Published in 2013
by
Christian Focus Publications Ltd,
Geanies House, Fearn,
Ross-shire, IV20 1TW, Scotland.
www.christianfocus.com
and
Porterbrook Network
215 Sharrow Vale Road
Sheffield, S11 8ZB
www.porterbrooknetwork.org

Cover design
by
Daniel van Straaten

Printed by
Bell and Bain, Glasgow

All rights reserved. No part of this publication may be reproduced, stored in a retrieval system, or transmitted, in any form, by any means, electronic, mechanical, photocopying, recording or otherwise without the prior permission of the publisher or a licence permitting restricted copying. In the U.K. such licences are issued by the Copyright Licensing Agency, Saffron House, 6-10 Kirby Street, London, EC1 8TS. www.cla.co.uk

CONTENTS

Introduction

Then they [the apostles] gathered around him [Jesus] and asked him, 'Lord, are you at this time going to restore the kingdom to Israel?' He said to them: 'It is not for you to know the times or dates the Father has set by his own authority. But you will receive power when the Holy Spirit comes on you; and you will be my witnesses in Jerusalem, and in all Judea and Samaria, and to the ends of the earth.'

After he said this, he was taken up before their very eyes, and a cloud hid him from their sight.

They were looking intently up into the sky as he was going, when suddenly two men dressed in white stood beside them. 'Men of Galilee,' they said, 'why do you stand here looking into the sky? This same Jesus, who has been taken from you into heaven, will come back

in the same way you have seen him go into heaven.'
(Acts 1:6-11)

Let's be honest: the ascension of Jesus is weird. It is
the story of a man who appears to be taken up into the
clouds. I remember reading the story with a friend who
is not a Christian. She looked at me with pity as if to say,
'You don't really believe this sort of wacky stuff, do you?'
I was about to object to her unspoken accusation when
I thought, 'Yes, actually, this is pretty weird'.

The two men, who were probably angels, do not help
matters. 'Why do you stand here looking into the sky?'
they say. Surely the answer is obvious! The apostles have
just seen a man taken up into the clouds. I think I'd be
looking up to see what happens next. The point, of course,
is that what happens next will take place on earth. Jesus
is sending the Holy Spirit to empower them to be His
witnesses. But at this point staring up into the sky doesn't
seem a surprising thing to do!

So the ascension *is* weird. But it can also feel a bit
disappointing. You may have had conversations that went
something like this:

'If God exists then why doesn't he make himself
known? Why doesn't he write a message in the sky?
Surely he could if he were God.'

'But he has made himself known. He sent his Son,
Jesus. Jesus is God among us. He made God known.'

'So you say. But how can I know that? Jesus died
a long time ago.'

Or perhaps like this.

'How can you be so confident there's life after death?'

'Because someone came back from the dead. The resurrection of Jesus is key to the claims of the Christian gospel. Our faith stands or falls on this historical event.'

'So how do you know that's what really happened and wasn't just a made-up story?'

'Because the tomb was empty and because eyewitnesses saw Jesus alive. And those eyewitnesses weren't gullible people desperate to believe. Thomas doubted the news until he saw and heard and touched Jesus for himself. And meeting the risen Jesus changed their lives. They went from hiding in fear from the authorities to boldly proclaiming the story of Jesus even when faced with persecution, imprisonment and martyrdom.'

'Yes, but someone coming back from the dead? There's no scientific proof for anything like that.'

Wouldn't evangelism be a whole lot easier if Jesus was still on earth? Imagine He was still living somewhere in Palestine so that people could go to see Him. Imagine that scientists had studied Him over the years and could verify that He was over 2,000 years old. Or imagine that Jesus Himself was on tour, performing miracles and preaching the gospel.

The ascension seems a bad strategy. It removes the key piece of evidence that substantiates the claims of Christianity. It's as if our best player by far was substituted just as the game was beginning.

In this book we want to show that the ascension is good news. In fact, there could be no salvation and no mission without the ascension. John Owen, the great

Puritan theologian, says: 'This assumption of our Lord Jesus Christ into glory, or his glorious reception in heaven, with his state and condition therein, is a principal article of the faith of the church – the great foundation of its hope and consolation in this world ... The darkness of our faith herein is the cause of all our disconsolations, and most of our weaknesses in obedience.'[1]

What was the immediate impact of the ascension event on the first disciples? 'Then they worshipped him and returned to Jerusalem with great joy. And they stayed continually at the temple, praising God.' (Luke 24:52-53) Worship, joy and praise. Their Lord and friend had been taken from them, but they understood enough of what had happened for it to produce in them worship, joy and praise.

More than that, Jesus says His physical absence is better for us than His continued physical presence. 'But very truly I tell you, it is for your good that I am going away. Unless I go away, the Advocate will not come to you; but if I go, I will send him to you.' (John 16:7) When He meets Mary Magdalene shortly after His resurrection, He says: 'Do not hold on to me, for I have not yet ascended to the Father.' (John 20:17)

As we understand the ascension, we will discover that it brings us great comfort. Diplomats and reporters sometimes talk about 'our man in Washington' or 'our man in Tokyo'. For Christians Jesus is 'our man in heaven'. He is there for us and on our behalf. He is our representative in heaven, securing our salvation by His presence.

---

1   John Owen, *On the Person of Christ*, *Works*, ed. William H. Goold, (Banner of Truth, 1850–53, 1965), vol 1, pp. 235 and 252.

But we will also discover that the ascension is a great challenge. The ascension is the enthronement of Jesus. He receives all authority and sends us out to declare that authority to the world. The ascension is the beginning of mission.

One
Ascended
Priest

Near where we live is the parish church of St Mary and St Martin in the village of Blyth, Nottinghamshire. Along the south side is a series of four stained-glass windows which date from around 1300. Each of the four windows consists of three pairs of stories. In each case the lower image is a story from the Old Testament while the image above depicts a New Testament story that fulfils the promise implicit in the Old Testament story. This is a medieval biblical theology in coloured glass.

Many of the pairings are predictable. Naaman being cleansed of leprosy in the River Jordan is paired with Jesus healing the leper in Mark 1. Isaac carrying wood up Mount Moriah is paired with Jesus carrying the cross. The Passover meal is paired with Jesus being stripped for crucifixion.

Two panes relate to the ascension. One shows Mary Magdalene grasping hold of the Risen Christ with Jesus saying, 'Do not hold on to me, for I have not yet ascended' (John 20:17). The second shows the ascension itself. Which Old Testament stories would you choose to match these New Testament fulfilments?

In the windows of St Mary and St Martin's the scene underneath Jesus saying to Mary, 'Touch me not for I am not yet ascended' is Abel's acceptable sacrifice (Gen. 4:4) and underneath the ascension itself is a picture of Abraham meeting the priest-king Melchizedek (Gen. 14:18). As we shall see, the medieval craftsmen who made these windows rightly identified the ascension as the fulfilment of all that sacrifice and priesthood represented in the Old Testament.

Consider the essential elements of the ascension story: 'He was taken up before their very eyes, and a cloud hid him from their sight.' (Acts 1:9) The core components are (1) being taken up and (2) being hidden by a cloud. We have seen these essential elements before in the Bible story. Ascending is not a new phenomenon. It is not without precedent. We have been set up for this moment.

The prophet Elijah was taken up into heaven. But 'Elijah went up to heaven in a whirlwind' and there is no mention of being hidden by clouds (2 Kings 2:11). The closer parallel is Moses at Mount Sinai and this is the allusion that the ascension fulfils. God had rescued the people of Israel from slavery in Egypt and brought them to Mount Sinai. At Mount Sinai God is going to make a covenant or contract with them. He is promising that He will be their God and they will be His people. At this point in the story we read: 'When Moses went up on the mountain, the cloud covered it' (Exod. 24:15).

Moses ascends the mountain on behalf of the people. He does this at the initiative of both God and the people. In Exodus 19 God tells Moses:

> Put limits for the people around the mountain and tell them, 'Be careful that you do not approach the mountain or touch the foot of it. Whoever touches the mountain is to be put to death' … Go down and warn the people so they do not force their way through to see the LORD and many of them perish. Even the priests, who approach the LORD, must consecrate themselves, or the LORD will break out against them.' (Exod. 19:12, 21-22)

In the next chapter the people themselves ask Moses to be their mediator. They have seen the glory of the LORD on the mountain and it fills them with fear. 'Speak to us yourself,' they say, 'and we will listen. But do not have God speak to us or we will die.' (Exod. 20:19)

People cannot come into God's presence. We are all corrupted by our sin and selfishness. And God is a holy God. The Bible describes Him as a consuming fire. His judgment burns against sin and we are all sinners. We are all rebels and God is the Lord against whom we have rebelled. God Himself says that He would *'break out against'* us (Exod. 19:22; 33:5).

So Moses ascends the mountain on behalf of God's people to come before God where He is hidden by a cloud.

This is exactly what happens at the ascension of Jesus: Jesus ascends on behalf of God's people to come before God where He is hidden by a cloud. The only difference is that Jesus does not ascend to the top of a mountain, but to heaven itself.

What happens next in the story of Moses? Moses is told to build a tabernacle, a tent which functions as a kind of portable temple. God gives Moses a plan for the tabernacle's construction and operation: 'Then have them [the Israelites] make a sanctuary for me, and I will dwell among them. Make this tabernacle and all its furnishings exactly like the pattern I will show you.' (Exod. 25:8-9) Exodus 25–30 describes these instructions at some length and Exodus 35–40 describes its subsequent construction. Moses is repeatedly told to build the tabernacle on the basis of what he has seen on the mountain. God says: 'See that you make them according to the pattern shown you on the mountain.' (Exod. 25:40; 26:30; 27:8)

Why does this matter? Why does God give such specific instructions? Because the tabernacle constructed in Exodus 35–40 is not the first. It is a copy. The writer of Hebrews says the Jewish high priests 'serve at a sanctuary that is a copy and shadow of what is in heaven. This is why Moses was warned when he was about to build the tabernacle: "See to it that you make everything according to the pattern shown you on the mountain."' (Heb. 8:5; cf 9:23)

The earthly tabernacle is a copy of the heavenly tabernacle. The earthly tabernacle recreates the mountain experience. In Exodus 33:9-11 the cloud envelopes the tabernacle whenever Moses meets with God just as the cloud enveloped the mountain when Moses met with God on Sinai. The earthly tabernacle is a kind of surrogate for ascending into the clouds. It replicates what will happen in heaven. It is not the real thing. The real action takes place in heaven.

God also tells Moses how the earthly tabernacle is to operate. The high priest is to act as a mediator between God and His people. The high priest will enter God's presence through sacrifice. Sin inevitably leads to death. Death is the just penalty for sin. So the only way that people can come before God is if something dies in their place. This is what sacrifice represents. When the tabernacle is completed it is consecrated through the sprinkling of sacrificial blood and a daily round of sacrifices begin (Exod. 29:38-46). The blood of sacrifice means the tabernacle can serve its function as a place where humanity can come before our holy God.

The so-called 'burnt offering' described in Exodus 24:5-8 and Leviticus 1 could be translated 'ascension offering'.[1] The Hebrew word comes from the verb 'to go up'. So it could simply mean 'to go up in smoke', but it could also have the sense of 'the sacrifice for going up'. In Exodus 24 this sacrifice prepares for the ascension of the seventy elders of Israel into the presence of God. 'Moses and Aaron, Nadab and Abihu, and the seventy elders of Israel went up and saw the God of Israel. Under his feet was something like a pavement made of lapis lazuli, as bright blue as the sky. But God did not raise his hand against these leaders of the Israelites; they saw God, and they ate and drank' (Exod. 24:9-11). The offering enables the representatives of God's people to ascend to share a meal in God's presence because God's hand is raised against the sacrifice in the place of His people. This is replicated in the tabernacle offerings (Lev. 1). During this offering the animal is burnt up and is turned into smoke that replicates the cloud of Mount Sinai. So the offering does not simply deal with sin, but deals with sin *so that* we can ascend into the presence of God.

It is not just sacrifices that are described in detail. God also gives specific instructions about the clothes the priest

1   Peter Leithart, 'Ministerial Conference Outline #1,' 2004, www.leithart. com/archives/000869.php.

must wear: he must wear a breastplate with twelve jewels that represent the names of God's people (Exod. 28:15-21). It is as if the priest brings the people of God into the presence of God.

Now come back to the ascension. Here is Jesus our mediator, our sacrifice. Here is His shed blood, the sacrifice to which all other sacrifices pointed. Here is our priest carrying our names. And He ascends into the clouds. But He does not come to the tabernacle – that was only a shadow, a picture. Nor does He even come to the mountain. No, He passes through the clouds into heaven itself.

What the priests did when they entered the tabernacle was a kind of *pre*-enactment of the ascension. We often talk about re-enactments – copies of significant events that communicate what they were about. It might be crime re-enactment that hopes to jog someone's memory about significant evidence. Or it might be a battle re-enactment that preserves the memory of heroism and sacrifice. What we have in the tabernacle was a *pre*-enactment – a copy of an event still to come that communicated something of what the ascension would involve.

- Moses is the mediator between God and His people; Jesus is the true mediator between God and His people.

- Moses ascends up a mountain into the clouds; Jesus ascends through the clouds into heaven itself.

- Moses is shown a copy of the heavenly tabernacle which he replicates on earth; Jesus ascends to enter the real thing, the heavenly tabernacle.

- The priest comes before God through the blood of sacrifice; Jesus ascends to come before God on our behalf through His own sacrificial blood.

- The priest comes into God's presence through a cloud of incense; Jesus passes through the clouds of heaven.

- The priest comes before God bearing jewels that represent the names of God's people; Jesus ascends to come before God on our behalf and in our names.

These parallels are not accidental. I might illustrate an idea by saying, 'It's a bit like playing football,' but the ascension is not simply 'a bit like' Moses going up Mount Sinai or 'a bit like' the tabernacle. Moses was more like an architect who makes a model of a building so everyone can see what the real thing will look like when it's built. The earthly tabernacle was constructed as an illustration of the heavenly tabernacle. That was its purpose. Its similarity to the ascension was not incidental – that was what it was made for. The tabernacle (and the temple that later replaced it) was designed by God to show us the significance of the death, resurrection and ascension of Jesus. The hundreds of years of daily sacrifices, plus the thousands of animals that were butchered along the way, were all instituted to help us understand the priestly work of Jesus.

Understanding the ascension of Jesus in the light of Mount Sinai and the Old Testament tabernacle is at the heart of the theology of the book of Hebrews.

The writer of Hebrews writes to encourage his readers not to turn back from following Jesus. Perhaps they are facing hardship and wondering if it is worth following

Christ. But perhaps, too, they are Jewish believers who miss the tangible presence of temple, priests and sacrifices. So the writer of Hebrews insists that Jesus is better. He is the reality to which all these things were mere pointers.

His message is this: 'Since we have a great high priest who has ascended into heaven, Jesus the Son of God, let us hold firmly to the faith we profess' (Heb. 4:14). It is an appeal to the ascension. Because Jesus has ascended into heaven, we can and must hold firmly to our faith. How does this work?

Central to his argument is his identification of Jesus as a true high priest. Jesus is truly human so He is able to sympathise with us just like the old covenant priests (5:1-10). The old covenant priests had to be Levites and descendants of Aaron whereas Jesus was from the tribe of Judah (securing His right to be the true king). The writer of Hebrews, however, connects Jesus with an older priesthood, the priesthood of Melchizedek who ministered to Abraham before the tribes of Israel even existed (5:6-10; 7:1-16). But his central argument is that God appointed Him as our priest (7:17-22).

Jesus is a better priest for two reasons. First, He is an eternal priest: 'Now there have been many of those priests, since death prevented them from continuing in office; but because Jesus lives for ever, he has a permanent priesthood. Therefore he is able to save completely those who come to God through him, because he always lives to intercede for them.' (7:23-25)

Second, He is a perfect priest who offers a complete sacrifice. 'Unlike the other high priests, he does not need to offer sacrifices day after day, first for his own sins, and then for the sins of the people. He sacrificed for their sins once for all when he offered himself.' (7:27) The old covenant priests had to keep making sacrifices because they themselves were sinners in need of atonement and because their sacrifices could never truly atone for sin. Their sacrifices were only ever intended as illustrations of Jesus the true lamb of God (9:9-10).

So Jesus is the true priest. This is what the writer of Hebrews demonstrates in chapters 5–7. And the argument turns on the cross and resurrection of Jesus. The cross is the true sacrifice that atones for sin and the resurrection establishes Jesus as permanent priest who lives forever as our intercessor.

> Christ presents Himself before God as our representative. His perfect manhood, his official character, and his finished work, plead for us before the throne of God. All that the Son of God as incarnate is, and all that He did on earth, He is, and did for us; so that God can regard us with all the favour which is due to Him. His presence, therefore, is a perpetual and prevailing intercession with God on behalf of His people, and secures for them all the benefits of His redemption.[2]

In chapters 8 and 9 the argument shifts. While the priest-hood of Jesus and the cross are still central, the focus moves to the true tabernacle and the ascension comes to the fore.

> Now the main point of what we are saying is this: We do have such a high priest, who sat down at the right hand of the throne of the Majesty in heaven, and who serves in the sanctuary, the true tabernacle set up by the Lord, not by a mere human being. (8:1-2)

---

2   Charles Hodge, *Systematic Theology*, (James Clarke, 1874, 1960), vol. 2, p. 592.

But when Christ came as high priest of the good things
that are now already here, he went through the greater
and more perfect tabernacle that is not made with human
hands, that is to say, is not a part of this creation. (9:11)

For Christ did not enter a sanctuary made with human
hands that was only a copy of the true one; he entered
heaven itself, now to appear for us in God's presence.
(9:24)

Jesus ascended into heaven 'to appear for us in God's
presence'. *Atonement was not complete until Jesus stood
before God on our behalf.* 'If he were on earth, he would not
be a priest, for there are already priests who offer the gifts
prescribed by the law' (8:4). 'They serve at a sanctuary that
is a copy and shadow of what is in heaven' (8:5). Jesus has
entered the heavenly original.

Jesus, our priest and mediator, appears in the presence
of God, bearing our names, as a memorial to God. He
is the sign, the reminder, the pledge, the guarantee that
we belong in the presence of God. Our presence before
God is as certain as Christ's presence before God. Our
salvation is safe and secure as long as Christ is in heaven.

This is why the ascension is such good news. This is one
reason why we would not want Jesus to leave heaven and
appear on earth, however convenient that might appear
for world evangelism. If Jesus were to leave heaven then
the pledge of our salvation would be removed. If *Christ*
is not in God's presence on our behalf then *we* are not in
God's presence.

Even on the final day, when Jesus does come to earth,
He does not leave heaven behind. He can never leave
heaven without jeopardising our salvation. Instead, He
brings heaven with Him to create a new heaven and a new

earth. He does not leave heaven to collect us and take us back to heaven. He brings heaven to earth. He brings the presence of God to the people of God so that the voice from the throne declares: 'Look! God's dwelling place is now among the people, and he will dwell with them. They will be his people, and God himself will be with them and be their God.' (Rev. 21:3) The new Jerusalem is structured as a tabernacle or temple.

Jesus ascended *for your salvation*. He is the memorial before God of your atonement. Can you see how powerful this is? Can you see how this is good news to those who doubt their salvation or feel the on-going weight of their sin or who sin in a spectacular way? In these moments we lift our eyes heavenwards and see Jesus in the presence of God on our behalf. He is the complete sacrifice who has taken away sin for ever. He is the eternal priest whose ministry never ends. While He stands in heaven you are secure in God's family.

The last lines of Augustus Toplady's hymn 'A debtor to mercy alone' are, 'More happy but not more secure, the glorified spirits in heaven.' The glorified spirits are those Christians who have already died and are now in the presence of God. They are more happy because their earthly sufferings are over. And they are completely secure. They are in God's presence far from any threat or temptation. But we are just as secure as they are because Jesus is in heaven on our behalf. Think of Jesus in the presence of God, bearing your name on His breast, securing your salvation. Jesus does not step out of the presence of God when we mess up.

In chapter 12 the writer of Hebrews brings our thoughts back to Mount Sinai:

> You have not come to a mountain that can be touched and that is burning with fire; to darkness, gloom and storm; to a trumpet blast or to such a voice speaking words that those who heard it begged that no further word be spoken to them, because they could not bear what was commanded: 'If even an animal touches the mountain, it must be stoned.' The sight was so terrifying that Moses said, 'I am trembling with fear.' (Heb. 12:18-21)

This is *not* our experience. The darkness, gloom and storm are gone. The trembling and fear are gone. But then so has the mountain. For we do not come to Mount Sinai, but to the heavenly reality to which it pointed. '[But] you have come to Mount Zion, to the city of the living God, the heavenly Jerusalem.' (12:22)

Jesus has ascended into heaven so that we can come to heaven. When we gather with God's people to worship God we join the worship of heaven. 'You have come to thousands upon thousands of angels in joyful assembly, to the church of the firstborn, whose names are written in heaven.' (12:22b-23a) When you sing out of tune each Sunday with elderly Mrs Jones on the organ or Bob getting his guitar chords muddled, you join the worship of heaven. We do this because we have come 'to Jesus the mediator of a new covenant, and to the sprinkled blood that speaks a better word than the blood of Abel.' (12:24) What makes our worship 'heavenly' is not the standard of the music, but Jesus our priest ascended in heaven on our behalf.

> In bringing many sons and daughters to glory, it was fitting that God, for whom and through whom everything exists, should make the pioneer of their salvation perfect through what he suffered. Both the one

who makes people holy and those who are made holy are
of the same family. So Jesus is not ashamed to call them
brothers and sisters. He says:

'I will declare your name to my brothers and sisters;
in the assembly I will sing your praises.'

And again,
'I will put my trust in him.'

And again he says,
'Here am I, and the children God has given me.'
(2:10-13)

The speech of the ascended Christ is addressed in two
directions: He addresses the congregation (proclaiming,
as the ascended prophet, the name of God) and He
addresses God (proclaiming His praises). The latter He
does explicitly 'in the presence of the congregation'. In
other words, when we gather to worship God, Jesus is our
worship leader. Hebrews 8:2 says we have 'a minister in
the sanctuary and in the true tabernacle, which the Lord
pitched, not man' (NASB). Jesus is our minister, leading the
worship of His people. Our praise rises to the presence of
God because Jesus rose to the presence of God. Our voice
is heard before God because His voice is heard before God.
Meanwhile through the Spirit He is present among us and
through the Spirit declares God's Word to us. Son and
Spirit bridge the gap between humanity and the Father,
not just in theory or in the future, but in our experience
in the present. Before the Father, Jesus says, 'Here am I,
and the children God has given me.' Jesus is there in the
presence of God and through the Spirit we are there with
Him so that our earthly praise ascends to heaven where it
mingles with the praise offered by the Son.

What does it mean to say Jesus is our cantor or choir master or worship leader? First, while He may not say the '1, 2, 3, 4' that counts in our voices, He does 'count in' our hearts, bringing them into time with the words we are singing. As the Spirit directs our thoughts to Jesus our hearts are warmed afresh and well up in praise to the Father for His grace. Second, the risen Jesus has paved the way for us to come before the Father. So our praises do not simply rise to the ceiling of the building in which we meet, but they rise by means of the blood of Jesus into the very presence of God. Your worship leader might be able to so lead your singing that the sound penetrates to the street outside, but only Jesus can enable our praises to penetrate up to heaven. And what counts is not the quality of our music, but the quality of His *mediation*. John Owen said:

> And what can be more glorious than this, namely, that the whole spiritual worship of the gospel, performed here on earth by the saints, is administrated in heaven by such a holy Priest … and … under his conduct we have by faith an entrance into the presence of God … [Worship] is performed in heaven. Though they who perform it are on earth, yet they do it, by faith, in heaven.[3]

What are we to do with the glorious truth of Christ ascended on our behalf? Listen again to the writer of Hebrews:

> Therefore, since we have a great high priest who has ascended into heaven, Jesus the Son of God, let us hold firmly to the faith we profess. For we do not have a high

---

3   John Owen, *The Nature and Beauty of Gospel Worship*, *Works*, ed. William H. Goold, (Banner of Truth, 1850–53), vol. 9, p. 65 & p. 77.

priest who is unable to empathise with our weaknesses, but we have one who has been tempted in every way, just as we are – yet he did not sin. Let us then approach God's throne of grace with confidence, so that we may receive mercy and find grace to help us in our time of need. (4:14-16)

'Therefore' and 'since' are both words that signal implications. 'We have a great high priest who has gone through the heaven, Jesus the Son of God.' This is reality. Since this is the case, what should we do? The writer introduces two things with the exhortation 'let us'. Given the ascension of our High Priest, let us do this.

First, 'let us hold firmly to the faith we profess.' The one who is in heaven on our behalf is a man. Jesus is humanity in the presence of God. So He can 'sympathise with our weaknesses'. Jesus is a man. But He is *our man in heaven*. His presence there gives us the confidence to press on without giving up.

Second, 'let us then approach the throne of grace with confidence, so that we may receive mercy and find grace to help us in our time of need.' Often we feel unable or unworthy to pray, but the foundation of prayer is the *fact* that Jesus *is us* in the presence of God. So while I may feel unworthy, the fact is that in Christ I appear in the presence of the Father. I can no sooner be removed from God's presence than Jesus can.

Two
Ascended King

When you went to bed last night Jesus was at work subduing His enemies. While you slept He was continuing to rule over the world. He was still at it when you woke up this morning and even now as you read this book. That is the outrageous claim of the ascension. It is outrageous because His rule is not recognised in His world. Open a newspaper and it is not full of how Jesus is reigning. Instead it is full of conflict and crime.

Yet the story of the ascension is the story of the enthronement of Jesus as king of the world. That is why the ascension is the climax of Luke's Gospel and the starting point for Luke's sequel, the book of Acts. Luke thinks the ascension is such good news that he tells the story twice!

MOVING TOWARDS THE ASCENSION OF GOD'S KING

From the beginning Luke's Gospel portrays Jesus as God's promised king. The angel Gabriel announces the birth of Jesus to Mary saying, 'He will be great and will be called the Son of the Most High. The Lord God will give him the throne of his father David, and he will reign over Jacob's descendants for ever; his kingdom will never end.' (Luke 1:32-33)

Luke's Gospel begins with two babies: John the Baptist and Jesus. Luke starts with the story of John's birth. It's the story of a childless couple who are promised a child in the temple and who respond in song (Luke 1:5-25, 67-79). Luke is reminding us of a similar story from the history of Israel. Many years before, another childless couple had gone to the temple and been promised a child (1 Sam. 1). The mother's name was Hannah and the child's name was Samuel who became one of Israel's greatest prophets. When Samuel was born, Hannah too responded in song (1 Sam. 2:1-10). Hannah's song was remarkably similar to another song sung at the beginning of Luke's Gospel, the song sung by Mary, the mother of Jesus (Luke 1:46-55). Luke tells the story of John's birth in a way that highlights its links to the birth of the prophet Samuel. The most important thing the prophet Samuel did was anoint Israel's greatest king, King David. Luke wants us to see John as the new Samuel. But if John is the new Samuel, what does that make Jesus? The new King David.

God made humanity to enjoy His rule. In Eden God's rule was a rule of provision and plenty, of peace, justice and freedom. But the Serpent persuaded Eve that God's rule was tyrannical, that God's rule was bad news. Adam and Eve believed the lie of Satan and so they rebelled against God's rule. They chose self-rule instead, but ended up enslaved. God now became their enemy. His rule now could only mean judgment and defeat.

But God was gracious. He promised that one day a son of Eve would defeat Satan and his kingdom (Gen. 3:15). God graciously began to restore His rule through His promise to Abraham of a people who would enjoy God's blessing once again. Abraham's family became the nation of Israel. After releasing them from the oppressive rule of Pharaoh in Egypt, God called them to live under His good rule, expressed in His law. In this way they were to show the world that God's rule is a good rule. They were to be the living proof that, contrary to Satan's lie about God, God's rule brings life, freedom, peace, justice and joy.

But, like Adam and Eve before them, the nation of Israel rejected God's rule. 'Everyone did as they saw fit' (Judg. 21:25b). Then they asked for a human king like the nations around them, even though God warned that such a king would become a tyrant. They were rejecting God as their king. As God had predicted, the reign of Israel's first king ended in disaster. So God chose a new king, David, who would prove to be Israel's greatest king. David gave the people rest from their enemies and God made a covenant with David, promising that one of his descendants would rule over God's people for ever (2 Sam. 7). As successive Israelite kings turned from God, divided the nation, led it into defeat, and ultimately brought it to the brink of ruin, this promise fuelled the hope of a coming King.

Isaiah held out the promise that a new David, a shoot from the stump of Jesse, would come and restore God's rule (Isa. 11:1-12). The earth would be filled with the knowledge of God (11:9), justice and peace would reign (11:1-5) and

God's people would be gathered in from the nations under His banner (11:10-11).

It is this hope about which the angel Gabriel speaks when he announces the birth of Jesus. Jesus is the son of David, David's heir, David's greater son. He is the one who will rule over God's people forever.

This is what causes Zechariah to burst into song when John the Baptist is born (Luke 1:68-69):

> Praise be to the Lord, the God of Israel, because he has come to his people and has redeemed them. He has raised up a horn of salvation for us in the house of his servant David.

Luke is not living in fairyland. He knows Israel is under occupation. Roman soldiers tramp the streets imposing Roman rule. Luke routinely dates the events he describes in relation to Jewish and Roman kings (1:5; 2:1; 3:1). Jesus is not some fantasy king living in another world. This is the real world of Roman occupation, a world in which any threat to the empire was quickly and efficiently crushed. But still Luke portrays Jesus as God's king.

In the first half of his Gospel Luke shows us the power of Jesus. The power of Jesus does not consist in the military machine that He has at His disposal. Instead with a word He rules the natural world, the spirit world, sickness and even death (8:26-56). At the climax of the first half of the Gospel Peter recognises that Jesus is the Christ, God's promised king.

The next thing that happens at this midway point in the story is that Jesus ascends a mountain where He is enveloped in cloud just as Moses had done on Mount Sinai.

About eight days after Jesus said this, he took Peter, John and James with him and went up onto a mountain to pray. As he was praying, the appearance of his face changed, and his clothes became as bright as a flash of lightning. Two men, Moses and Elijah, appeared in glorious splendour, talking with Jesus. They spoke about his departure, which he was about to bring to fulfilment at Jerusalem. Peter and his companions were very sleepy, but when they became fully awake, they saw his glory and the two men standing with him. As the men were leaving Jesus, Peter said to him, 'Master, it is good for us to be here. Let us put up three shelters – one for you, one for Moses and one for Elijah.' (He did not know what he was saying.) While he was speaking, a cloud appeared and covered them, and they were afraid as they entered the cloud. A voice came from the cloud, saying, 'This is my Son, whom I have chosen; listen to him.' When the voice had spoken, they found that Jesus was alone. The disciples kept this to themselves, and did not tell anyone at that time what they had seen. (Luke 9:28-36)

Jesus ascends into the clouds to receive glory. On the mountain 'the appearance of his face changed, and his clothes became as bright as a flash of lightning' (9:29). 'This is my Son' is an allusion to Psalm 2, which is itself an allusion to God's covenant with King David in 2 Samuel 7. Jesus is being acclaimed as king. It is a pointer to what will happen at the end of the story when Jesus ascends through the clouds into heaven to receive glory.

At this point the movement of the story changes direction. The focus of the ministry of Jesus has been Galilee, but now Jesus heads towards Jerusalem. Luke says: 'As the time approached for him to be taken up to heaven, Jesus resolutely set out for Jerusalem.' (9:51) It

is a striking phrase. The time that is approaching is the
time of His ascension. This is where the story is going. The
climax of the story will be God's king enthroned in glory.
But the way to heaven is via Jerusalem. The way to glory
is via the cross.

Jesus could have been enthroned as God's king without
the cross. He had the credentials. He was entitled. He was
from the line of David. He had authority over every area of
life. He could have put the world right through His Word
of power. But where would that have left His people?

Announcing the coming of Jesus, John the Baptist had
said: 'The axe is already at the root of the trees, and every
tree that does not produce good fruit will be cut down
and thrown into the fire.' (Luke 3:9) But the axe had not
fallen. Jesus came, but He did not bring judgment. In fact
Jesus eats with the enemies of God (5:27-32), so John has
to send a delegation to check whether Jesus is the real
thing (7:18-23).

Now God's king is advancing towards Jerusalem. Surely
this is the moment when He deposes Herod and throws
out Pilate. Surely now He will defeat God's enemies. But
instead Jesus is the one who is defeated. He is cast out of
this world onto the cross. He is judged.

God's rule is a rule of peace, justice, joy and freedom.
But not if you're an enemy of God. For rebels against God's
rule the restoration of His rule means judgment and defeat.
But here is the good news: when the king comes He comes
not to judge, but to be judged. He is judged even though
He has done no wrong. He is judged in the place of His
people. One day He will come in glory and triumph. One
day He will wrap up history and judge all humanity. That

will happen at what we call His second coming. But at His first coming He is the one who is judged. He dies our death. He bears the judgment we deserve so we can go free.

Only once when Jesus has redeemed His people from sin and death through His death on their behalf can He ascend to glory. This is what the disciples on the road to Emmaus don't get. 'We had hoped he was the one to redeem Israel,' they say (Luke 24:21). But what Jesus has to show them from the Scriptures is that God's king had to die to redeem His people. 'Did not the Messiah have to suffer these things and then enter his glory?' (24:26)

The disciples at the end of Luke's Gospel (24:21) and the beginning of Acts (1:6) expected the coming of God's kingdom to be a geographic reality involving national renewal. But God's purposes were always much bigger. God's king will rule over the whole earth and gather a people from every nation. But His route to His rule is via the cross so that His coming rule is good news to all who put their faith in Him.

Looking at the ascension from above
Imagine a television documentary which starts with an underwater shot of the body and feet of a bird seen from below the water line. Then the camera moves slowly up, bursts through the surface of the water so that now you look down on an elegant swan swimming across a lake. Or imagine taking off in a plane on a grey, drizzly day. To begin with your plane climbs up through the gloom and fog. But then suddenly you emerge into brilliant sunshine and an ocean of puffy, white cloud.

That is the kind of movement we make as we move from Luke 24 and Acts 1 to Daniel 7. Luke describes the ascension from below. This is the ground level view and we see one ordinary-looking person rise into the clouds. Daniel describes the ascension from above. He shows us what happens on the other side as Jesus moves through the clouds – not into earth's upper atmosphere, but into heaven.

Daniel himself, of course, sees all this hundreds of years beforehand in a dream. But Jesus alludes to Daniel's dream to refer to himself and to describe what will happen at the climax of His life (Luke 22:66-71). Daniel 7 seems to have been one of the key Old Testament passages that shaped how Jesus understood His identity and mission.

In Daniel's dream 'four great beasts, each different from the others, came up out of the sea.' (v. 3) The first is like a lion with the wings of an eagle. The second is a flesh-eating bear. The third is a winged leopard with four heads. The fourth beast is 'terrifying and frightening and very powerful. It had large iron teeth; it crushed and devoured its victims and trampled underfoot whatever was left.' (v. 7) It has ten horns which are supplanted by a little horn with 'the eyes of a human being and a mouth that spoke boastfully.' (v. 8)

Then Daniel sees 'the Ancient of Days' on a flaming throne from which flows a river of fire. He is surrounded by thousands of attendants. 'The court was seated', we are told, 'and the books were opened.' (v. 10) The fourth beast is slain and the other three are stripped of their power. Then Daniel says:

> In my vision at night I looked, and there before me was one like a son of man, coming with the clouds of heaven. He approached the Ancient of Days and was

led into his presence. He was given authority, glory and sovereign power; all nations and peoples of every language worshipped him. His dominion is an everlasting dominion that will not pass away, and his kingdom is one that will never be destroyed. (vv. 13-14)

An angel interprets the dream for Daniel: 'The four great beasts are four kings that will rise from the earth. But the holy people of the Most High will receive the kingdom and will possess it forever – yes, for ever and ever' (vv. 17-18). The fourth beast, we are told, is different because its empire encompasses the known earth. The little horn is a king of this empire who 'will speak against the Most High and oppress his holy people and try to change the set times and the laws.' (v. 25) The four beasts are probably the successive empires of Babylon, Persia, Greece and Rome. But, since the Persian empire was an alliance of the Medes and Persians, the beasts could be the Babylonians, Medes, Persians and Greeks, with Antiochus Epiphanes, the Greek king who desecrated the Jerusalem temple in 167 b.c., being the little horn. Whatever the chronology, the main point is clear: the kingdoms of this world will all be superseded by the kingdom of God. The interpretation of the dream ends:

But the court will sit, and his [the little horn's] power will be taken away and completely destroyed forever. Then the sovereignty, power and greatness of all the kingdoms under heaven will be handed over to the holy people of the Most High. His kingdom will be an everlasting kingdom, and all rulers will worship and obey him. (vv. 26-27)

Consider again the moment when this happens and how it is described: 'There before me was one like a son of man, coming with the clouds of heaven. He approached the Ancient of Days and was led into his presence. He was given authority, glory and sovereign power' (vv. 13-14). This moment is the ascension of Jesus.

In Acts 1 the angels tell the disciples that Jesus 'will come back in the same way you have seen him go into heaven' (Acts 1:11). In other words, at the end of history Jesus will return on the clouds. But in Daniel 7 the Son of Man is not moving *from* heaven *to* earth. In Daniel 7 He comes 'with the clouds' into the presence of the Ancient of Days. The movement is through the clouds *from* earth *to* heaven. So Daniel 7 describes what happens at the ascension, not what will happen at the return of Christ.

The 'Son of Man' was the normal phrase that Jesus used to describe Himself. In Daniel's dream the Son of Man comes with the clouds of heaven and is given all authority by God. This is what happens on the other side of the clouds as Jesus disappears from the sight of His disciples. He enters heaven, comes before the Ancient of Days and, as the triumphant, risen Christ, is given 'authority, glory and sovereign power'. This is His enthronement. The king promised by the angel Gabriel at the beginning of Luke's Gospel (1:32-33) is enthroned as He is taken up into heaven at the end of Luke's Gospel (24:51).

We have already seen that the second half of Luke's Gospel (from 9:51 onwards) is built around Jesus' journey to Jerusalem. This journey comes to a climax when Jesus enters Jerusalem as her king (19:28-40).

Luke's portrayal of Jesus as the new David is especially strong in the birth stories and then it drops from view. But

Luke has not lost sight of the story. What happens is that, like David, Jesus wanders on the periphery with a small band of followers while being persecuted by the powerful. Then, like David, Jesus enters Jerusalem in triumph before ascending His throne. It's at this point the allusions to David return. As Jesus enters Jerusalem on a donkey He is hailed as the king promised in Psalm 118:26: 'Blessed is the king who comes in the name of the Lord!' (Luke 19:38; see also 13:35). That He comes on a donkey is an allusion to Zechariah 9:9 and the coming of God's promised king. In 20:41-44 Jesus uses Psalm 110 to show that the son of David could be the greater Messiah. David spent much of his life on the margins as the anointed-but-not-yet king before he was finally enthroned and made Jerusalem his capital. Jesus spends much of His life on the margins as the anointed- but-not-yet king before being acclaimed king as He enters Jerusalem.

But the real climax of the journey is at the end of the Gospel when Jesus *leaves* Jerusalem through His ascension (24:50-53). This is His true 'triumphant entry' as He enters heaven as the triumphant king with authority over heaven and earth. That's the difference between David and Jesus. In Acts 2:34 Luke records Peter saying: 'David did not ascend to heaven, and yet he said, "The Lord said to my Lord: 'Sit at my right hand.'"' David is not the ultimate king, he is not the king of the world, because he did not ascend to heaven. His throne was only in Jerusalem. Jesus is the king of Israel *and* the king of the world.

Earlier in his Gospel Luke has already hinted that the kingship of Jesus extends to the world beyond Jerusalem. If Luke was only interested in Jesus as the new David then he could have stopped this genealogy at Luke 3:31

with the mention of David. But he takes it back to Adam (3:38). And then in the story of Jesus being tempted in the wilderness in Luke 4:1-13 Luke does a double replay. First, he shows Jesus replays the story of Israel being tempted in the wilderness for forty years. Jesus is in the wilderness for forty days and responds to Satan's temptations by quoting Deuteronomy, the book from the wilderness wanderings. And secondly, Luke shows Jesus replays the story of Adam being tempted by Satan in the Garden of Eden. Jesus is both Israel in the wilderness and Adam in the garden.

The Jews believed the redemption of the world would come through Israel. Adam has sinned and through his sin judgment had come upon all people. But God had chosen Israel so that through Israel salvation would come to all people. Except that Israel had sinned – archetypally in the wilderness when they built the golden calf. Instead of being the solution, Israel had made matters worse. So now, before the world could be redeemed through Israel, Israel herself had to be redeemed.

But now someone has come in the wilderness to be tempted by Satan and He has not sinned. Therefore Jesus is the new David come as Israel's king to rescue Israel.

The redemption of Israel will lead to the redemption of the world. So Jesus is also the new Adam come as *the world's* king to rescue *the world*. What was Adam told to do in the garden? He was told to rule. He was, as it were, the king of the earth, ruling under God, bringing peace and prosperity to the world. But he rejected God, and Adam's rule turned to tyranny. The earth was cursed and humanity was judged. In the wilderness temptation Satan comes to Jesus and 'takes him up' in a pseudo-ascension to offer Him the kingdoms of the world if He will rule under the banner of the Serpent (Luke 4:5-7). But this time the true Adam rejects the rule of the Serpent and chooses a route to the throne in submission to God.

So Jesus is the new Adam, the new David, the new King, the Saviour of the world whose rule will bring peace and prosperity. And where will the King of the world be enthroned? Not in Jerusalem. If he's enthroned in Jerusalem then He is just Israel's king. No, Jesus is enthroned in heaven as the king of the whole world.

THE ASCENDED KING REIGNS THROUGH THE MISSION OF HIS PEOPLE

So the ascension describes the enthronement of Jesus as God's promised king. The ascended Jesus was given all authority when He came with the clouds of heaven before the Ancient of Days. But what does that look like in twenty-first-century Sheffield or New York or Lagos? How does Jesus reign in the world today? Is it all just theoretical? Or all just heavenly? Is it a make-believe reign?

The answer is that Jesus reigns when people submit to the gospel and He extends His reign throughout the earth through the mission of His people.

Matthew does not talk about the ascension from an earthly perspective. He does not tell the story of Jesus rising up into the clouds. But at the end of Matthew's Gospel Jesus does allude to Daniel 7 and anticipates His heavenly enthronement as God's ascended king. The fact of the ascension is there, front and centre, even if the story is absent. This is how Matthew concludes his Gospel:

> Then Jesus came to them and said, 'All authority in heaven and on earth has been given to me. Therefore

go and make disciples of all nations, baptising them in
the name of the Father and of the Son and of the Holy
Spirit, and teaching them to obey everything I have
commanded you. And surely I am with you always, to
the very end of the age.' (Matt. 28:18-20)

'All authority in heaven and on earth has been given to
me' is an allusion to Daniel 7. Jesus is anticipating His
ascension. Shortly He will come on the clouds to the
Ancient of Days and receive 'all authority'. This then is the
basis for the mission of His people. The 'therefore' at the
beginning of the Great Commission is crucial: it is because
Jesus has been enthroned that He tells His disciples to go
to all nations. The ascension is the foundation of global
mission; mission is the logic of the ascension.

Moreover, what is it that Jesus tells the apostles to
do? They are to 'make disciples' by baptising people and
teaching them 'to obey everything I have commanded
you'. In other words, they are to call on people to submit
to the authority of Jesus. They are to call on people to obey
the commands of the ascended king. The mission of the
church is an exercise of authority. We call on people to
submit to the government of Christ through the gospel.

Jesus exercises His rule on earth through the
proclamation of His Word – just as God has always
reigned through His Word. 'The Church's proclamation of
the Gospel becomes thus the *sceptre*, as Clement of Rome
called it, through which the risen and ascended Christ
rules over the nations and all history.'[1] We are ambassadors
of Christ bringing an authoritative pronouncement from

---

1   T. F. Torrance, *Space, Time and Resurrection*, (The Handsel Press, 1976),
     p. 121.

the king. When we proclaim the gospel we are heralds of a coming king. It is as if we go to the citizens of a country and say that a king is coming who rightly claims their allegiance. Those who currently rule them are usurpers and tyrants. But the true king is coming and He will be king. He will reign.

This is what takes place in evangelism. We declare that Jesus is king and that Jesus will be king. The earliest encapsulation of the Christian message was 'Jesus is Lord' – confessed at a time when the rest of the world was declaring Caesar to be Lord (Rom. 10:9). Jesus has been given all authority by the Father and one day every knee will bow before Him. If people acknowledge His lordship now, they will experience His coming rule as blessing, life and salvation. If they reject Him, they will experience His coming rule as conquest, death and judgment.

We live in a culture where choice is everything and value judgments are relative, in which I decide what is right for me. The declaration of Christ's kingship cuts right across this. We do not invite people to make Jesus their king; we tell people that Jesus is their king. We do not invite people to meet Jesus; we warn people that they will meet Jesus as their conquering king, either through the gospel or as their judge on the final day. We do not offer people a gospel invitation; we command people to repent and submit to the coming king. Of course we do this graciously and gently (1 Pet. 3:16). We cannot force or manipulate repentance. But one day everyone will bow the knee before Jesus one way or another (Phil. 2:9-11).

Much of our evangelism takes an individual you-and-God approach: you have sinned, your sin cuts you off from God, but Jesus removes the consequences of sin so you can know God again. There is nothing incorrect about this story. But the Bible tells a much bigger, fuller story. It is the story of God creating a new humanity, reasserting His liberating rule over the world, and bringing it to a climax in the triumph of His Son and the renewal of creation.

The danger of the you-and-God message is that I remain at the centre. I am the almighty consumer, shopping around for what suits me best with God providing the best option for my religious life. God serves my spiritual needs while Tesco serves my grocery needs. And the customer is always right. But the ascension puts Jesus firmly at the centre of my life and our world.

The ascension is a public act in the sense that it impacts the public realm. It is not a private event that affects only Jesus and His friends. We should not think of Jesus as a spiritual king who is not the king of the earth. We should not live as if Jesus simply sneaked off the scene, not wanting to cause a fuss, or as if one day Jesus decided to withdraw from public life and so He took the elevator up to heaven. In His absence, His people keep their heads down with Jesus as king of their hearts until they too can take the elevator to join Him in heaven. We should not reduce the kingship of Jesus to a private affair for a ghetto people.

As we have seen, Jesus disappearing into the clouds is only half the story. He emerged on the other side into heaven as the king to whom all authority has been given. Nothing could be more momentous for life on earth. This story creates a people who proclaim Him boldly in the face of hostility. His kingship continues to be disputed by the world, but we have seen in the ascension the story of His enthronement. It is the enthronement of Jesus over all authorities. It is the beginning of the end for the empires of this world – for Caesars and Czars, for presidents and generals. It is an event that is to be proclaimed publicly to all nations. It does not create a church bunkered down in a ghetto, but a church that confidently proclaims the coming of Earth's king.

If we spiritualise the ascension and get Jesus safely diffused and dissolved into the heavens, then He no longer seems a threat to the rulers of the world. Rather, we can neatly divide the regions of authority between the spiritual and the worldly. We can build a wall between public and private truth which protects us from the claims of God. A spirituality Jesus allows the kings of the world to run free without restraint from the church, and allows the church to run after the things of the world without the downdraft pressure of the return of the embodied Jesus.

> A continuing incarnation, however, enthrones Jesus in direct relationship to the world and its ruler. There is a real, human king who reigns over the world from heaven. A man who once walked among us is on the throne, and he is not aloof from the affairs of his realm below. All other powers on earth, therefore, are merely temporary and derived.[2]

THE ASCENDED KING PROTECTS THE MISSION OF HIS PEOPLE

We see the reign of Christ wherever His Word is proclaimed and trusted. If your friend responds with faith to an evangelistic course then Christ's reign has been extended. If you talk about how you became a Christian with a colleague at work then Christ's reign is being

---

2   Gerrit Scott Dawson, *Jesus Ascended: The Meaning of Christ's Continuing Incarnation*, (P&R/T&T Clark, 2004), p. 55.

announced. If someone is baptised then Christ's reign has taken visible form in their life. If you make a choice to obey Christ's command in the face of temptation or you hold on to the promises of Christ in the face of adversity then Christ's reign is present in history. Your church is the place in your neighbourhood where Christ's reign can be seen and experienced.

But it is not easy, is it? Did you hope for more? Were you hoping that Christ's reign would mean the defeat of His enemies and the vindication of His people? Were you hoping for a blaze of glory, something everyone could and everyone would have to acknowledge? That is coming. That is how it will be when Christ returns.

But in the meantime it is not easy. It was not easy for the newly formed church in Ephesus. For one thing, the power of the Roman Empire was everywhere. The city of Ephesus was the most important city in the Roman province of Asia with most of the produce from Asia Minor passing through it en route to the rest of the empire. A wide road lined with columns on both sides ran from the city down to the harbour. Everywhere you looked were the symbols of Roman rule – just like the posters that line our streets and the adverts that fill our television screens. It certainly did not look like the kingdoms of this world had been stripped of their power.

Not only was the power of Rome all too evident in Ephesus, but Ephesus was a hotbed of occult activity. When Paul first preached the gospel there he was met with an unusual amount of demonic activity (Acts 19). When believers who had practised sorcery publicly burnt their scrolls – probably spells and incantations – the value was 50,000 drachmas. That is about 50,000 days work.

No doubt the sense of evil and threat was palpable for those first Ephesian believers. How were they to proclaim Christ in such a hostile context?

Paul tells them he prays that God would give them 'the Spirit of wisdom and revelation' so they would know God better, so they would know the glorious inheritance that awaits them and so they would know the great power that is theirs in Christ.

> That power is the same as the mighty strength he exerted when he raised Christ from the dead and seated him at his right hand in the heavenly realms, far above all rule and authority, power and dominion, and every name that is invoked, not only in the present age but also in the one to come. And God placed all things under his feet and appointed him to be head over everything for the church, which is his body, the fulness of him who fills everything in every way. (Eph. 1:19-23)

What do weak and marginalised Christians need to know? They need to know that Christ has ascended, that God has seated Him in the heavenly realms, that He is far above all rule and authority, power and dominion.

But Paul goes further. Christ has been appointed head over everything *'for the church'*. His ascension into glory and His enthronement as king is for the church. It is for you.

In Matthew's Gospel Jesus promises 'I am with you always' as His people go in His name to make disciples of all nations (Matt. 28:18-20). He will be with us in mission. The same promise is given to us as we protect the church through church discipline. The ascended Christ will be with us and grant us His authority when we gather in His name to confront unrepentant brothers and sisters (18:15-20; see also 1 Cor. 5:4-5).

Christ has been given all authority so He can exercise that authority to protect and prosper His church. He looks down from heaven, as it were, to see what His church needs and to ensure those needs are met. He guides the advance of the gospel and the growth of the church.

THE ASCENDED KING PROVIDES FOR THE MISSION OF HIS PEOPLE

The shadowing of events in heaven and events on earth, of Daniel 7 and the story of Acts, does not stop with Jesus disappearing from view in Acts 1:11. The events of Pentecost are also part of the fulfilment of Daniel's dream. From His throne in heaven the ascended king sends the Holy Spirit on His people to empower them to extend His reign through the proclamation of His Word. The climax of Peter's Pentecost sermon is an exposition of the ascension.

> Exalted to the right hand of God, he has received from the Father the promised Holy Spirit and has poured out what you now see and hear. For David did not ascend to heaven, and yet he said, 'The Lord said to my Lord: "Sit at my right hand until I make your enemies a footstool for your feet."' Therefore let all Israel be assured of this: God has made this Jesus, whom you crucified, both Lord and Christ. (Acts 2:33-36)

David did not ascend to heaven, but David's greater Son *has* ascended to heaven. God has exalted Jesus, making Him Lord over His enemies and making Him Lord and Christ. And this is the explanation of the outpouring of God's Spirit that prompted the sermon. Peter ascribes the coming of the Spirit to the ascended Christ. The work of the Spirit throughout the story of Acts takes place at the command of the ascended Christ. In a striking phrase, for example, Peter tells a bedridden man, 'Jesus Christ heals you' (9:34). In Acts 26:23 Paul claims that Moses predicted 'that the Christ would suffer and, as the first to rise from the dead, would proclaim light to his own people and to the Gentiles.' Notice the agency of Christ in the mission of the church: it is Christ who proclaims light to Jews and Gentiles.

Christ ascends into heaven at the beginning of the book of Acts, but He is not then absent from the story. On a number of occasions He intervenes from heaven and these prove to be key moments in the story.[3]

In Acts 7 Jesus appears to Stephen: 'Stephen, full of the Holy Spirit, looked up to heaven and saw the glory of God, and Jesus standing at the right hand of God' (v. 55). This comes at the climax of Stephen's long speech to the Jewish authorities, and it leads to his martyrdom and to the persecution of the church that scatters the believers into Judea and Samaria. The gospel begins to move beyond Jerusalem in accordance with the plan outlined by Jesus in 1:8: 'you will be my witnesses in Jerusalem, and in all Judea and Samaria, and to the ends of the earth.'

In Acts 10–11 Peter sees 'heaven opened' (10:11) and hears a voice 'from heaven' (11:9). In his vision a sheet of unclean food is 'let down to earth' (10:11) before being 'pulled up to heaven again' (11:10). This experience of heaven sends him beyond the confines of Judaism as he

---

3   This section draws upon the work of Matthew Sleeman in *Geography and the Ascension Narrative in Acts*, (CUP, 2009), and 'The Ascension and Heavenly Ministry of Christ,' in *The Forgotten Christ: Exploring the Majesty and Mystery of God Incarnate*, ed. Stephen Clark, (IVP/Apollos, 2007), pp. 140-89.

goes to proclaim the gospel to the house of the Gentile Cornelius. The mission of the church begins to move to the ends of the earth.

In Acts 9 the ascended Jesus speaks to Paul on the road to Damascus. He then calls to Ananias in a vision and speaks of a further revelation to Paul: 'I will show him how much he must suffer for my name' (v. 16). This subsequent vision sets the agenda for Paul's mission to the Gentiles in the second half of Acts. Paul's recounting of this vision in Acts 22:17-21 provokes the mob and leads to his arrest and journey to Rome which then dominates the final chapters of Acts. Before King Agrippa, Paul says, 'I was not disobedient to the vision from heaven' (Acts 26:19). Speaking from heaven, the ascended Christ has set the agenda for Paul's life and for the book of Acts. Matthew Sleeman concludes, 'It becomes apparent that, throughout Paul's ministry, it has been *the heavenly Christ* throughout Acts proclaiming light to both Jew and Gentile.'[4]

Paul explains the early church's experience of the ascended Christ in Ephesians 4: 'But to each one of us grace has been given as Christ apportioned it. This is why it says: "When he ascended on high, he took many captives and gave gifts to his people"' (vv. 7-8). It is the ascended king, having received all authority at His ascension, who dispenses gifts to His church. 'So Christ himself gave the apostles, the prophets, the evangelists, the pastors and teachers, to equip his people for works of service, so that the body of Christ may be built up …' (vv. 11-12).

---

4   Matthew Sleeman, 'The Ascension and Heavenly Ministry of Christ' in *The Forgotten Christ*, p. 154.

Conclusion

The ascension establishes the age of mission, both because the king is on the throne and because the king is absent. Jesus leaves this earth to allow those who belong to the old age time to repent. 'The ascension means that Jesus has withdrawn Himself from history', says T. F. Torrance, 'in order to allow the world time for repentance.'[5] Judgment has been passed, but sentencing is deferred. 'The Lord is not slow in keeping his promise, as some understand slowness. Instead he is patient with you, not wanting anyone to perish, but everyone to come to repentance' (2 Pet. 3:9). Gerrit Scott Dawson puts it like this: 'Jesus' withdrawal makes necessary the mission of the church to the world, but also makes room for the world to receive the mission of the church and come to believe the gospel.'[6]

The kingdom is 'now', fully and totally. Christ has been given all authority. But the ascension creates a hiatus when the kingdom of God is 'not yet' the only kingdom on earth. The ascension creates an overlapping period between the ages in which it seems as though Jesus is not in control. As Christians living in the old age as citizens of the new age, it can be hard to detect the rule of the king and easy to become despondent when we see His rule rejected. Jesus' kingdom is not the only one in town claiming authority. One tendency in these times is to seek to create visible forms of His rule on earth, claiming we are building the kingdom here to challenge and to win over the kingdoms of the earth. But the ascension challenges both the secular

5 T. F. Torrance, *Royal Priesthood*, (T&T Clark, 1993), pp. 59-60.

6 Dawson, *Jesus Ascended*, p. 145.

attempts to build alternative kingdoms and the church's attempts to build the kingdom on earth.

An ascended Jesus reminds both the kingdoms of the world and the church that this world is incomplete and unfinished. And not just unfinished, but un-finishable without the return of Jesus. We cannot bring the world to perfection. The Enlightenment project of human progress is bound to fail. The ascension puts us in our place. It is Jesus who reigns, not us. And it is Jesus who will bring in God's new world at His return, not us through our scientific ascent or church programmes of social renewal, as valuable as they are.

So the ascension checks any tendency for Christians to claim too much authority on earth. One day the kingship of Jesus will be 'revealed' (Luke 17:30). Our role is not to create God's kingdom, but to model the reality of heaven and proclaim His kingship, even if this means suffering.

> Without adequate recognition of the real absence of Christ, the church itself has no real absence; knowledge of his presence renders it prone to self-glorying and to illusions of worldly power, to making martyrs of others rather than walking the path of martyrdom itself.[7]

Where do we see Christ's rule and His power? The gospel is the rule of Christ manifest in the world. It is the way in which He brings justice and righteousness to the world. His rule is seen most clearly where people proclaim the gospel and most align their lives to the gospel story. The king rules as people take up their cross and follow Him in the hope of resurrection glory. The kingdom does not depend on us, but we do get the privilege to model the

---

7   Douglas Farrow, *Ascension Theology*, (T&T Clark, 2011), p. 70.

heavenly rule of Jesus as we take the gospel to others in word and deed.

Luke, as we have seen, has two accounts of the ascension. In the second version in Acts he tells us that 'two men dressed in white' appear. '"Men of Galilee," they said, "why do you stand here looking into the sky? This same Jesus, who has been taken from you into heaven, will come back in the same way you have seen him go into heaven."' (Acts 1:11) At the end of his Gospel Luke makes no mention of the angels and their message. Why is that? It is because the ascension story at the end of Luke's Gospel frames that Gospel: the story begins with the coming of Jesus from heaven and ends with His departure back 'up into heaven' (Luke 24:51). In Acts the ascension again frames Luke's story, but this time it is a different story. The story begins with Jesus being 'taken from you into heaven' and it will end with Jesus coming back from heaven. Except that the book of Acts does *not* end with the return of Jesus from heaven. That is because this story is not over yet. Luke wants us, his readers, to realise *we* are part of this on-going story – the story of the mission of the church.

The existence of small pockets of Christians living as communities united in the gospel on mission to the world – these are the sign that one day Jesus will transform the kingdom of the earth. At the end of history heaven cries: 'The kingdom of the world has become the kingdom of our Lord and of his Messiah, and he will reign for ever and ever.' (Rev. 11:15)

Three
Ascended Man

The Reformed tradition has often discussed the work of Christ under His roles as our Prophet, Priest and King. So, with chapters on Jesus as our ascended Priest and ascended King, readers may be anticipating a chapter on Jesus as our ascended Prophet. It would certainly be possible to write such a chapter, perhaps beginning with John 16:7-15 or Ephesians 4:7-13, with Jesus ascending so He can send the Spirit to enable His people to know and proclaim His Word.

But one of the greatest wonders of the ascension is that a *human being* is now in the presence of God. Human flesh is now with God. Central to the doctrine of the ascension is the wonder of an ascended man. We use the word 'wonder' in both its senses – something that amazes us and something that puzzles us. The ascended man both amazes and puzzles us. First the puzzle: Where is Jesus?

The puzzle of the ascended man

Before we address this question, forget the ascension of Jesus for a moment. What connotations does the language of 'ascent' have in our culture? What do people mean by 'the ascent of man'?

Sometimes it is a synonym for evolution. Man has ascended above the animals and the sign of our ascent is our superior intellectual development. Or, the ascent of man is a synonym for civilisation. Our ascent is our move from primitive cultures to 'high' culture. Or consider the term 'higher being'. In the television programme *Star Trek* higher beings are those who have evolved to a point where they have left their bodies behind and become pure mind or pure love. They speak to Captain Kirk from the ether or even communicate thought-to-thought through telepathy. Ascension in our modern culture is an ascent of the mind that often involves a move away from bodily existence – a movement from the physical to the spiritual or from the bodily to the mental.

This is how many people think about the ascent of Jesus. In this view the ascension of Jesus means He is now spiritually everywhere in a disembodied sense. Perhaps He has become one of *Star Trek's* higher beings – pure mind or pure love unconstrained in space by a body. We remake the ascension of Jesus in the image of our notions of human ascent instead of understanding human ascent in the image of Christ's ascension.

THE SCANDAL OF AN ASCENDED MAN

In John 6:61-62 we read: 'Aware that his disciples were grumbling about this, Jesus said to them, "Does this offend you? Then what if you see the Son of Man ascend to where he was before!"' To understand the nature of this offence we need to see how this ascension statement connects with what Jesus has been saying.

> Jesus said to them, 'Very truly I tell you, it is not Moses who has given you the bread from heaven, but it is my Father who gives you the true bread from heaven. For the bread of God is the bread that comes down from heaven and gives life to the world.'
>
> 'Sir,' they said, 'always give us this bread.'
>
> Then Jesus declared, 'I am the bread of life. Whoever comes to me will never go hungry, and whoever believes in me will never be thirsty …'
>
> At this the Jews began to grumble about him because he said, 'I am the bread that came down from heaven.' They said, 'Is this not Jesus, the son of Joseph, whose father and mother we know? How can he now say, "I came down from heaven"?' …
>
> Jesus said to them, 'Very truly I tell you, unless you can eat the flesh of the Son of Man and drink his blood, you have no life in you. Whoever eats my flesh and drinks my blood has eternal life, and I will raise him up at the last day.' …
>
> On hearing it, many of his disciples said, 'This is a hard teaching. Who can accept it?'
>
> Aware that his disciples were grumbling about this, Jesus said to them, 'Does this offend you? Then what if you see the Son of Man ascend to where he was before!' (John 6:32-35, 41-42, 53-54, 60-62)

John 6 is about the *descent* of Jesus *from heaven* and an explanation of the saving power of His death. Jesus is the bread of life that comes down from heaven. The scandal is that the life-giving bread of heaven is a human person. The life-giving bread of heaven has come down in human flesh. Hence the strange language of eating the flesh of Jesus, a picture of believing that this person in human flesh can give us eternal life. This would have scandalised most Greeks since they thought of salvation as an escape from the flesh. It would have been just as scandalous to Jews to suggest Yahweh the divine Saviour would become flesh and bring salvation through being enfleshed.

But a scandal just as significant is coming: human flesh will *ascend* into heaven. The life-giving bread that descended from heaven and became human flesh will ascend back to heaven *as human flesh*. The scandal is not just that God has left heaven to be 'enfleshed' on earth, but that God will return to heaven in the flesh. As John ('Rabbi') Duncan, the Scottish theologian and missionary, said, 'The dust of the earth sits on the throne of heaven.'[1] Human flesh becomes a permanent fixture in heaven (a scandal to Greeks) and a permanent fixture for the Son of God (a scandal for Jews).

As early as the third century Origen advised Christians troubled by the idea of literal bodily ascension to understand it in 'a mystical sense ... as an ascension of the mind rather than of the body'.[2] Origen was the first of many Christian theologians who have ignored or rejected

---

1   John Duncan, cited by L. Ligon Duncan in the introduction to Derek Thomas, *Taken Up to Heaven: The Ascension of Christ*, (Evangelical Press, 1996), p. 11.

2   Origen, *On Prayer*, 23.2; cited in Douglas Farrow, *Ascension Theology*, p. 17.

the bodily ascension of Jesus. Just as many have questioned the physical and bodily resurrection of Jesus in the vain hope of making Christianity acceptable to the modern world, so some have rejected or marginalised a physical and bodily ascension. The ascension is 'spiritualised' so that to ascend is to transcend the physical world in favour of a mental world. His physical absence is not felt because physicality is unimportant.

Many early theologians could accept that Jesus was divine, but struggled to accept that He was truly human. They suggested He merely appeared in human form or that the divine Christ temporarily resided in the body of human Jesus. It is often said that in modern theology the opposite is true: modern theologians have no problem accepting the humanity of Jesus, but they question whether He was truly God. There is much truth in this. But, when it comes to the ascension, the humanity of Jesus remains a contested area. 'It is still the humanity of Christ over which we are prone to stumble,' comments Douglas Farrow, 'and what is required today more than ever is a doctrine of the ascension that does not set his humanity aside.'[3]

The Enlightenment developed a secular version of this unfleshed ascension. It made much of the ascent of man, but made it an ascent of the mind. In other words, the modern world has a doctrine of the ascension. But instead of the ascent of human flesh into the presence of God, it is the ascent of the mind through progress in history. Ascension becomes a general principle of human progress. Jesus, if He is retained at all, becomes a model

3   Douglas Farrow, *Ascension and Ecclesia*, (T&T Clark, 1999), p. 13.

for us to follow. 'One way or another,' bemoans Farrow, 'Jesus-history has been made over into the manifestation of a universal principle or pattern, Jesus himself becoming the dispensable element.'[4]

However, the Bible stubbornly refuses to allow the story of Jesus to be read in this way. The ascension is the story of a body moving to heaven. It is not escape from the bodily realm, but the entry of humanity – in our physical-ness – into the heaven, the sphere of God. Far from diminishing the importance of the body, the ascension is the ultimate affirmation of bodily existence. The Son of God Himself has a body – not as an historical convenience, but as a permanent presence in heaven. In the face of these spiritualised or abstract versions of the ascension we must assert the physical and bodily ascension of Jesus. Human flesh is now with God. Nick Needham says:

> This is not to say that his risen, ascended humanity hasn't been glorified. It has. So there are differences between his earthly humanity and his ascended humanity, but that doesn't alter the fact that he is still human. He has a glorified humanity, not a glorified something else … The ascended Christ is still a human being and that he will remain a human being for all eternity - an exalted and glorified human being, yes, but a human being with a recognisable human body.[5]

We can assume that Jesus in heaven does not have a body because we think we know what heaven is like – a disembodied, ethereal sort of place. But we should

---

4   Farrow, *Ascension and Ecclesia*, p. 256.
5   Nick Needham, 'Christ Ascended for Us – Jesus' Ascended Humanity and Ours', *Evangel* 25:2, (Summer 2007), p. 42.

not let our notions of heaven shape our understanding of Christ and His ascension. Instead we should let our understanding of Christ shape our notion of heaven. The body of Jesus is in heaven. If that means we need to think about heaven in a new way then so be it.

People often think of heaven as a place above the earth, a space beyond the clouds, with hell as an 'underworld' below the earth. Certainly the first Christians used the language of up and down, of ascent and descent. But they were very capable of using metaphor. We must not assume they naïvely thought of the world as a three-story building with heaven above and hell below. When we talk about someone moving 'up' in the world, no-one thinks this means they have moved to live on a mountain.

It is better to think of the heavenly and earthly as two separate planes that intersect. The up and down imagery of the Bible captures the separateness. The heavenly realms transcend earthly existence. But there is also an intersection between the two. Heaven is not a far away place at the corner of the universe. Angels do not need to teleport to appear to people. They simply step from one dimension into another. Jacob dreamed of a ladder connecting earth and heaven at a place he called 'the gate of heaven' (Gen. 28:10-19). At the transfiguration the heavenly realm transfigured the earthly realm. Jesus says to Nathaniel: 'I tell you the truth, you shall see heaven open, and the angels of God ascending and descending on the Son of Man.' (John 1:51) Or think of it like Narnia. In his series of children's stories, *The Chronicles of Narnia*, C. S. Lewis imagines another world that is not our world, but which intersects with our world so that it is sometimes possible to move between them. Lewis himself said Jesus was like an actor who slips between two curtains, but appears to slip into one of its folds.[6] Jesus disappears, as it were, into a 'fold' in space. Heaven and earth are like different dimensions in one universe – two dimensions that inhabit the same space.

Jesus goes away, but He is also near. So is He in our universe or outside it? Simple spatial descriptions of the relationship between heaven and earth can confuse us. We must not think of space as a fixed receptacle. It is not an empty jar containing the stuff of the universe. If we think of space like this then Jesus, since He is embodied, must be somewhere in the jar. Or, if He is not in our jar, then He must be in another jar, presumably in another universe.

But instead of viewing space as a fixed receptacle, we should think of it from a relational point of view. Space exists or opens up through relationships between things. Take the tabernacle as an example. When the fabric is attached to the poles in an open area of desert, from a receptacle view of space, the inside of the Holy of Holies exists in the same spatial dimensions as the outside. It is just a space within a larger space marked out by some temporary walls. It differs from the outside *quantitatively* by degrees of measurable distance (it's a few yards away from the space outside). But viewed relationally, the Holy of Holies was far more than this. It was *qualitatively* different from the camp that surrounded it. That is, it was relationally different. It was God making a *place* for Himself in our world from which He could relate to His people and through which they could relate to Him. He did it through His saving acts, the provision of the

---

6   Cited in J. I. Packer, *Knowing Christianity*, (Eagle, 1995), p. 190.

covenant promises, the sacrificial system and priesthood. Through these things a *place* was opened up in the desert for God and humanity to relate. There wasn't just a simple inside and outside, differentiated only by co-ordinates on a mathematical grid. There were holy and unholy places. The presence or absence of God always defies spatial definitions. He inhabited the temple, but no house can hold Him. Space opens up in accordance with what is in it. In theoretical physics we find a similar view of space. Time, motion and space are all measured from the point of view of the observer. The flow of time and the movement of objects through space all happen with some reference to the position of the observer. This was Einstein's point. If we think about the measurement of the motion of an object through a space, it never happens in a vacuum. We have to include the position of the points the measurements are made from relative to the object measured and the relative motion of the world on its axis and the rotation around the sun. The movement and the space are themselves subject to the relationships between objects. This is simply to say that space, time and motion are not absolute fixed entities, but are constituted through relationships between things. T. F. Torrance says, 'We must not abstract the notion of space from that which is located in space – for space concretely considered is place, but place not abstracted from purpose or content, and place not without ends or purposeful limits. Time and space must both be conceived in relational terms.'[7]

The relational nature of creation and space should not surprise readers of the Bible who know that it was created,

---

7   T. F. Torrance, *Space, Time and Resurrection*, pp. 130-1.

and is continually sustained, by God's Word. Space exists as a Trinitarian act between the divine persons, the Father creating through the Word and breathing life through the Spirit.

Torrance argues that we are better off speaking of *place* rather than space. A place is room made for something in terms of the thing that inhabits it. A space just describes a receptacle. Torrance speaks of heaven as God's *place* instead of God's *space*. In this way we do not ask, '*where* is it?' but rather, 'what makes it open up and stay open?' The answer is God's nature and His purposes. God does not inhabit a space, but makes His own *place*. God's place is His Trinitarian relational nature. When that nature enters our *place* it transforms it. The receptacle or mathematical view of space is something specific to human *place*. It is part of the creation. When God enters our place He transforms it through His character and action – heaven breaks in. God does this by taking on spatial, earth-bound qualities. Ultimately this is seen in the incarnation where God takes on human flesh in order to enter our *place*.

This means that to ask the question 'Where is Jesus?' makes no sense. It is an earth-bound question. It is already to assume that the answer can be given in terms of mathematical co-ordinates. It presupposes He must be somewhere in our time and space. But Jesus has ascended to be with God. He is in God's place. His location is relationally determined. He is with the Father or before the Father or at the right hand of the Father – all relational designations of location. But just as God's presence with us transforms our places, so the presence of Jesus through the ascension changes the place of God. The place of God is reconstructed to include space because a man must inhabit it. God admits space into His place because space is a necessary part of humanity's place and now a man is in the place of God. This opens the way for the creation of a new creation which unites heaven and earth, and in which God dwells with His people.

THE ABSENT CHRIST IS PRESENT THROUGH THE SPIRIT

The role of the Spirit is key in this. If you ignore the role of the Spirit then Jesus can only be with us at the expense of His embodiment. But the embodied Christ who is absent in that body is present with us *through the Spirit.* John 7:37-39 says:

> On the last and greatest day of the festival, Jesus stood and said in a loud voice, 'Let anyone who is thirsty come to me and drink. Whoever believes in me, as the Scripture has said, rivers of living water will flow from within them.' By this he meant the Spirit, whom those who believed in him were later to receive. Up to that time the Spirit had not been given, since Jesus had not yet been glorified.

The Spirit is given through the ascension so that the glorified Christ is present with His people to revive and refresh them. It is the Spirit who enables us to talk about both the presence and absence of Jesus without contradiction. John Calvin says, 'What, then, our mind does not comprehend, let faith conceive: that the Spirit truly unites things separated in space.'[8] As Douglas Farrow puts it, 'The ascended Lord is not everywhere ... but he *is* everywhere accessible.'[9]

---

8   John Calvin, *Institutes of the Christian Religion*, trans. F. L. Battles, ed. J. T. McNeill, (Westminster/SCM, 1961), 4.27.10.

9   Farrow, *Ascension and Ecclesia*, p. 178.

If Jesus is not absent as the promise and sign of a new creation then we have no real hope. The rule of Jesus would be the rule we see on earth now in the church. And that would be a big disappointment for anyone who has read the Bible's promises of God's new world!

Imagine that you are living under a repressive regime. But there is a king in exile who promises a new life. You are part of a resistance cell spreading the news of this coming king. Imagine that you suddenly discovered the king was one of your companions. What disappointment! You had hoped that when the king arrived everything would be made new. But here he is and nothing much has changed. No, his absence is good news. It means there is still hope. It means a day of freedom is coming.

But what if the king was only absent and you never heard from him. You might well give up hope. Had he forgotten about you? Did he even exist? You would want him to be in touch. You want him to send an envoy to bring his word, to remind you of his coming, to equip you to endure.

Jesus is that king who is coming to make the world new. His absence is good news because it means this world is not it. There is more to life. There is a world made new on the horizon. But He is not only absent. The Holy Spirit is His envoy in the world. The Spirit speaks the words of Christ to us. He reminds us of His coming and He empowers us to endure.

The illustration does not quite do justice to the reality. The Holy Spirit is not another being; both Jesus and the Spirit are one God with the Father. We encounter the Son when we encounter the Spirit. Because the three are one we encounter Christ when we encounter the Spirit. Yet, because the one is three, the Spirit is not the Son. So Jesus is both really present and really absent.

Meeting the absent Christ through the Spirit at the communion table

The nature of the ascended body of Christ was central to discussions of the Lord's Supper at the time of the Reformation. Indeed this was perhaps the main issue over which the mainstream reformers disagreed. The Lutheran tradition wanted to interpret Jesus' words 'this is my body given for you' literally (Luke 22:19). They rejected the Catholic idea of transubstantiation in which the bread and wine are physically transformed into the body and blood of Christ. But they argued that at the ascension the humanity of Jesus moved beyond the confines of space and became ubiquitous (everywhere). In this way the body of Christ could really be said to be present in the bread and wine.

The Reformed tradition led by John Calvin argued that the ubiquity of the ascended Christ compromises His continuing humanity. It dissolves, as it were, the humanity of Jesus into His divinity. It is not a real human body if it is not located in a particular location. 'As we have proved by firm and clear testimonies of Scripture, Christ's body was circumscribed by the measure of a human body. Again, by His ascension into heaven he made it plain that it is not in all places, but when it passes into one, it leaves the previous one.'[10] How can Christ's body be visible in one place (in heaven), asks Calvin, and invisible or hidden in another (in the communion bread)? 'Where is the very nature of a body,' he asks, 'and where its unity?'[11] He talks

---

10   Calvin, *Institutes*, 4.27.30.

11   Calvin, *Institutes*, 4.27.29.

of 'that insane notion … that His body was swallowed up by his Divinity'.[12] Another Reformed theologian, Francis Turretin, puts it like this: 'We maintain that Christ went up locally, visibly and bodily from the earth into the third heaven or seat of the blessed above the visible heavens not by a mere withdrawal of his visible presence or familiar intercourse, but by a true and local translation of his human nature.'[13]

Calvin argued there was no need to take the phrase 'this is my body' literally. That is not how Scripture uses language elsewhere. When the Bible says Christ is a rock we do not conclude that He is a lump of inanimate stone. In the same way, when Jesus says 'this is my body', we should not think of the bread as human flesh. If the bread is literal flesh and the blood is literal blood then, says Calvin, we are left with the absurd idea that Christ's body and blood are separated.[14]

Christ clearly says He will leave His disciples: 'I came from the Father and entered the world; now I am leaving the world and going back to the Father.' (John 16:28) It is hard to evade the implication that He is not present! If this is interpreted as meaning Christ changes His state so He becomes present everywhere, asks Calvin, why then does He talk of sending the Holy Spirit as His replacement?[15] And why does the New Testament speak of us waiting for Christ as it does in Acts 3:21 and Philippians 3:20-21?

---

12   Calvin, *Institutes*, 4.27.29.

13   Francis Turretin, *Institutes of Elenctic Theology*, (P&R, 1994), vol. 2, p. 367.

14   Calvin, *Institutes*, 4.27.18, 23.

15   Calvin, *Institutes*, 4.27.26.

But if the body of Christ is absent when we take communion, does that then mean we are left with a mere memorial?

Calvin's answer is an emphatic 'No'. We really do encounter Christ in the bread and wine. We really do feast on Him so that we are nourished – and not just by having our memories jogged. The ascended Christ may be absent in body, but He is present by the Spirit. The distance between the ascended Christ and ourselves is collapsed by the Holy Spirit.

> The sharing in the Lord's body, which, I maintain, is offered to us in the Supper, demands neither a local presence, nor the descent of Christ, nor an infinite extension of His body, nor anything of that sort; for, in view of the fact that the Supper is a heavenly act, there is nothing absurd about saying that Christ remains in heaven and is yet received by us. For the way in which He imparts Himself to us is by the secret power of the Holy Spirit, a power which is able not only to bring together, but also to join together, things which are separated by distance, and by a great distance at that.[16]

So the communion meal expresses our union with Christ and so reinforces it to our experience. Calvin says:

> The bond of this connection is therefore the Spirit of Christ, with whom we are joined in unity, and is like a channel through which all that Christ himself is and has is conveyed to us. For if we see that the sun, shedding its beams upon the earth, casts its substance in some measure upon it in order to beget, nourish, and

---

16   John Calvin, *The First Epistle of Paul the Apostle to the Corinthians*, ed. David W. Torrance and Thomas F. Torrance, trans. John W. Fraser, (St Andrew's Press, 1960), pp. 246-67.

give growth to its offspring – why should the radiance of Christ's Spirit be less in order to impart to us the communion of his flesh and blood?[17]

It is not that Christ comes down to us in the Lord's Supper. Rather, by the Spirit, we ascend to be with Christ in the Lord's Supper.[18]

When is Jesus?

We can turn the question 'Where is Jesus?' inside out in two ways. First, the question is not simply 'Where is Jesus?' but 'When is he?'

Suppose you are going to watch a movie with some friends and you agree to meet in the foyer of the cinema. Two or three of you are gathered round and someone says, 'Where's Charlie?' This 'Where?' question is really a 'When?' question. You all know where Charlie is – he's on his way to the cinema. You might guess the route he will be taking. He will be somewhere along Brightside Lane, maybe waiting at one of the sets of traffic lights. So the real question is, 'When is he going to arrive?' Or suppose you are making the dinner or reading a book and someone asks, 'Where are you up to?' Again the spatial question is as much a temporal question. It is a variation on the question, 'How far through the task are you?' or 'When do you think you will finish?'

In the same kind of way, the spatial question, 'Where is Jesus?' easily morphs into temporal questions, 'Where is He up to?' and 'When will He arrive?'

We might say then that Jesus is in the future. He is physically present in the new creation. In that sense, we

---

17   Calvin, *Institutes*, 4.27.12.

18   Calvin, *Institutes*, 4.27.31.

will catch up with Him. There is some truth in this, but it is too easy to conceive of it in the wrong way. The problem is we think of the future as 'the present later on', but that does not do justice to the Bible's language of 'coming' and 'return'. It is not that we eventually come to Jesus as we travel along the road of history. He comes to us. Jesus is not part of this age further along. He is part of a new age, a different time. We can talk about Him being in the future as long as we realise it is a whole new future that has already begun through His resurrection and ascension. Just as the 'space' of heaven is a dimension we do not (yet) experience, so the 'time' of the new age is a dimension we do not (yet) experience. It will come to us. Or rather, Jesus will bring it to us.

In the meantime we wait. The ascension leaves us waiting on the return of Jesus from a time and place we do not yet fully experience, but which through the Spirit we inhabit.

From the perspective of this world the ascension seems unbelievable. But the ascension is an act of another world, of the new world, of the new age. The Risen and Ascended Christ represents reality. He is the truly real. His body is the beginning of the new creation.

Where are we?

The ascension question may be, 'Where is Jesus?' but the ascension also poses a question to us, 'Where are we?' And it poses it to us not so much as a question of metaphysical speculation, but as a missional challenge.

The obvious answer is that we are on earth, but the New Testament also claims that we are in heaven with Jesus: 'God raised us up with Christ and seated us with

him in the heavenly realms in Christ Jesus'; (Eph. 2:6)
'Our citizenship is in heaven' (Phil. 3:20).

Does this mean that one day we will be zapped up from
this earth to heaven – like Captain Kirk being beamed up
to the Starship Enterprise? No, our hope is for a renewed
earth (Rom. 8:19-21), for life in God's presence on a new
earth (Rev. 21:1-5). We straddle two worlds: we live in
this world as citizens of heaven.

We should not think that the future will involve an
obliteration of the earthly by the heavenly. In this view
the 'now' of the kingdom of God becomes somewhere
else other than here and the 'not yet' becomes the establishment of the kingdom through a final destruction of
the earth. Eternity is viewed as an ethereal existence on
clouds.

But the climax of the story is not the replacement of
earth with heaven or heaven with earth, but the unification
of heaven and earth as heaven descends to earth in a new
creation (Rev. 21:1-5). This unification of heaven and
earth is anticipated and established in the incarnation,
death, resurrection and ascension of Jesus. Jesus causes the
new age to erupt into the old age.

So earth is our home, but it is not our home – not
yet. Earth is our home, but not this earth in its current
state with its current regimes. Earth will be our home, but
only when it is united with heaven in a new creation. As
a result we live in the present life like citizens of a foreign
country. We live like pilgrims passing through.

This means the ascension checks our worldliness. Why
would we lay up treasure on earth when we can lay up
eternal treasure in heaven? In this sense the ascension
impacts our spending decisions. What we spend on

homes, clothes, cars or holidays will be shaped by the ascension. The ascension reminds us that our citizenship is in heaven, our inheritance is in heaven, our treasure is in heaven and our Saviour is in heaven. Everything we have of real value is in heaven. Samuel Rutherford, the seventeenth century Scottish theologian, said, 'My heart is not my own, [Christ] has run away with it to heaven.'[19] In this perspective the treasures of earth lose their lustre. What is more, our heavenly treasure is secure. So we can take risks with property, pay-checks and pensions – not because God guarantees to prevent bad things happening in our lives on earth, but because everything we have of real value is in heaven and it is there securely.

Who are we?

The world is full of ascension language. Things can be 'on the up', but they can also take a 'downward turn'. We want to 'rise' in our career. Charities try to 'lift' people out of poverty. We want to 'rise above' our problems and avoid a 'downward spiral'. People are 'lifted' out of obscurity and 'rise above' the crowd. We love stories of successful people because we want to emulate the 'heights' to which they have 'risen'. Or perhaps we want secrets that will bring them 'down' in our estimation so we do not feel ascension-failures by comparison.

The hope of ascension is a basic human aspiration. We want to rise above difficulties and reach our full potential. Most people want to end the day with a sense of achievement. The appeal of television programmes like *The X-Factor* is the opportunity for ordinary people to lift

19   Cited in I. D. E. Thomas, *A Puritan Golden Treasury*, (Banner of Truth, 1977), p. 47.

themselves out of obscurity into the limelight to receive glory and honour. We are gripped by rags to riches stories; the Cinderella story is deeply embedded in our culture. We want to become what we were always meant to be or what we were born to be. Every human being wants to 'ascend'.

What has the ascension of a man into heaven done for our humanity? Who are we in the light of the ascended man?

The ascension of Jesus is the ultimate rags to riches story. A child born in a barn becomes the king of the world. But it is not His story alone. It is the story of the restoration of humanity. The story of Jesus is the story of His people. All believers participate in this rags to riches story. We ascend to become who we were born to be.

Humanity was made by God to be a royal family. Psalm 8:5-8 says: 'You have made them a little lower than the angels and crowned them with glory and honour. You made them rulers over the works of your hands; you put everything under their feet: all flocks and herds, and the animals of the wild, the birds in the sky, and the fish in the sea, all that swim the paths of the seas.' We were made in the image of God to be kings over God's world. We were crowned with glory and honour. God is the great king and His children image His glory and honour to the world through their kingship under Him. God ruled by His Word in creating the world, subduing the chaos and forming it into a habitable home for the display of His glory. Adam and Eve as God's image-bearers act in His likeness, filling and subduing the earth (Gen. 1:28), naming creation (Gen. 2:19-20). Humanity was to represent God's character to the world through our ruling stewardship of creation.

This role of stewarding creation as God's royal children was carried out through the Holy Spirit. At creation the Spirit hovers over the formless void (Gen. 1:1-2). The Word of God that orders the chaos comes on the breath of the Spirit of God (Ps. 33:6). The Spirit breathes life into a lump of clay to create the first man (Gen. 2:7).

This image of God in humanity becomes marred and twisted when we rebel against God's rule. Now we exercise our rule over the world in destructive and self-serving ways. We rejected God's Word and opted instead for a self-referential rule by our own words. As a result, creation itself is subjected to frustration (Rom. 8:19-21). Our status as God's royal children is lost.

Ever since then we have had an inbuilt hunger to return to the throne. This is the source of our drive towards ascension. This is the reason why our language is littered with references to ascension. We know we are not what we are meant to be and we are not what we are born to be.

But our own attempts at ascension are sinful. They follow the pattern of the Fall, attempting to engulf the throne of heaven in the glory of man. Our role as kings was to be worked out through the task of stewarding creation for God's glory. The tower of Babel was the archetypal attempt to ascend to heaven to 'make a name for ourselves' (Gen. 11:4). Humanity exercises rule over creation – building a tower from clay – to conquer heaven in the name of humanity. The tower was built under the continuing influence of the Serpent's words, 'you will be like God' (Gen. 3:5). The story of the tower of Babel is the story of everyone's daily attempts to ascend: to work for our glory and to restore our kingship on our terms, to control our world for our glory. We have not escaped

the lies of Satan. His words still enthral us and direct our
stewardship of creation.

But God promises to restore humanity through His
people, Israel. This hope becomes further focused in the
king. Israel's king is to embody what it means to rule over
the world and restore creation (Ps. 72). King Solomon,
filled with wisdom, begins to look like something
approaching a restored Adam. In 1 Kings 4:29-34 his
wisdom includes flora and fauna. At the height of his rule
justice and fruitfulness flourish under God's blessing. But
Solomon's reign ends in disappointment as he pursues
foreign wives and foreign gods.

Isaiah 11:2, however, speaks of a coming Spirit-
empowered king who will reign in righteousness: 'The
Spirit of the LORD will rest on him – the Spirit of wisdom
and of understanding, the Spirit of counsel and of power,
the Spirit of knowledge and of the fear of the LORD.'
Isaiah speaks of a man who fulfils all that humanity was
designed to be, and who will be God's agent of restoration
for both humanity and creation.

As we have seen, Luke portrays Jesus as the Spirit-filled
king and the new Adam. In Luke 3:22 He receives the
Spirit at His baptism and hears the words of Psalm 2:7
spoken to God's king, 'You are my Son'. Jesus is 'the Son
of Adam' (Luke 3:38) who, filled with the Spirit, rejects
the temptation of Satan in the wilderness (4:1-13). Like
the first Adam this man has been declared the Son of God
(3:38) and equipped with the Spirit (4:1). Satan 'takes him
up' in pseudo-ascension and offers Him the kingdoms of
the world if He will rule under the banner of the Serpent
(Luke 4:5-7). It is the same offer he made to the first
Adam, to ascend to a throne under the Serpent. But this

time the true Son of God rejects ruling under the Serpent and chooses a route to the throne through submission to, and dependence on, God. The temptation story signals Jesus as the beginning of the new humanity who will fulfil its royal identity under God.

In 1 Corinthians 15 Paul presents Jesus as the true Adam (v. 22). He quotes from Psalm 8 which, as we have seen, describes humanity's rule over creation (v. 27). Christ restores our rule over creation by defeating His enemies (vv. 24-26) and becoming subject to God (vv. 27-28). Royal order is re-established: humanity in Christ ruling creation under God. T. F. Torrance says, 'The humanity of Jesus, although risen and triumphant over all decay and corruption, was fully and truly human, and indeed more fully and truly human than any other humanity we know, for it was humanity in which all that attacks and undermines creaturely and human being is vanquished.'[20]

Hebrews 2 also quotes from Psalm 8. Hebrews reminds us that God made everything subject to humanity (vv. 5-8). But it also acknowledges that 'at present we do not see everything subject to them [humanity]' (v. 8). But what we do see is Jesus, the new Adam: 'But we do see Jesus, who was made a lower than the angels for a little while, now crowned with glory and honour because he suffered death, so that by the grace of God he might taste death for everyone.' (v. 9)

The ascension of Jesus is the foretaste of the ascension of a new humanity to our royal status. 'And just as we have borne the image of the earthly man, so shall we bear the image of the heavenly man.' (1 Cor. 15:49)

---

20 T. F. Torrance, *Space, Time and Resurrection*, p. 127.

Those in Christ will once again be what we were meant to be and what we were born to be. Douglas Farrow says, 'Redemption does not mean the prising apart of creation to liberate what is divine in it, but rather the prising open of creation to the Spirit of God that it might be filled with divine glory … Salvation does not make us something other than human, but makes us rather to *be* human in another and truer way.'[21] Nick Needham says:

> Who is the one who is a true and perfect human being? It is the Lord Jesus Christ. So how do I define human nature and its capacities? Well, surely from what I find in Christ. Jesus Christ is the true definition of humanity. And at what point in Christ's life do we set our marker and say there is the final perfect definition of what humanity is – the new born baby Jesus, the teenager Jesus, the full grown man. No, we have to go on through Christ's public ministry, his passion, his death, his resurrection, his ascension into heaven. In other words, it is the man Jesus in his final condition: ascended, glorified, exalted who finally stands before us as the perfect definition of humanity. It is only in the exalted Christ that human nature comes to its full bloom, its full flowering, its final development of powers and capacities. If I want to see what human nature is ultimately capable of I do not look at my own stunted, twisted, deformed, diseased, shattered and pathetic shell of humanity. No, I look at the man Christ Jesus, risen from the dead and exalted to the right hand of the Father. That is real humanity, human nature according to God's final definition and purpose. That is human nature brought to its ultimate maturity of grace and glory.[22]

---

21 Farrow, *Ascension and Ecclesia*, p. 83.

22 Needham, 'Christ Ascended for Us – Jesus' Ascended Humanity and Ours', p. 47.

What does the royal status of restored humanity in Christ look like now? Christians rarely look royal in this world and the restored creation is yet to be revealed in all its glory (Rom. 8:18-25). We feel powerless and out of place in the old age. This is where the doctrine of the ascension can help us. The ascension secures our royal identity and locates it with Jesus in the presence of the Father. Far from the ascension and absence of Jesus being a pause on the delivery of our royal identity, it is the event that secures it. Because of the ascension we are seated at the right hand of the Father (Eph. 2:6).

In the present our life is currently hidden with Christ (Col. 3:1-3). Until the revelation of the sons of glory at the return of Jesus we express our royalty in the power of the ascension and through the pathway of the ascension. The power of the ascension is the Holy Spirit. On the day of Pentecost the completion of humanity through the crowning of Jesus coincides with the restoration of humanity through the giving of the Spirit. And the pathway of the ascension is the cross. It is by taking up our cross and following Jesus that our royal status is shown in this world. Jesus demonstrated His kingship by walking the road of suffering now through the cross before receiving glory. Until our glory is revealed, restored humanity looks like crucified humanity in the sense of people who embrace the sacrifice, submission, self-denial and service modelled in the cross.

The gospel declares that humanity is remade in the image of the glorified human Jesus. It is the gospel that makes us truly human, reclothes us in glory, fills us with the Spirit and seats us with the ascended Christ. It follows that restored humans will demonstrate their royal status by living in line with the gospel story. Death and resurrection is the true pattern of restored humanity. 'Here is a trustworthy saying: If we died with him, we will also live with him; if we endure, we will also reign with him.' (2 Tim. 2:11-12a)

THE BODILY ASCENSION AND THE MISSION OF THE CHURCH

As the ascended king Jesus sends us to proclaim His reign to the world through the power of the Spirit. As the ascended Man Jesus completes our renewed humanity. We call people to be truly human and find their identity in the true Man who has blazed the trail into the presence of the Father. By faith we are united to His death, resurrection and ascension. Our life and mission as Christians needs to be *'ascensional'*.

There is not much discussion of the ascension in the burgeoning literature on missional church. But without a theology of bodily ascension a functional or accidental theology can take its place. In particular, if we spiritualise the ascension, we can think our role is to be Christ's presence on earth. There is a lot of talk today of 'incarnational mission' or 'incarnational ministry'. For some people this is simply a way of affirming that we must love people as Jesus loved people and serve people as Jesus served people in their context.

But there is a dangerous tendency within some of this talk of incarnational ministry, a tendency to think our role is to be the presence of Christ on earth. We can think Jesus leaves His body behind and re-enters the world in a disembodied form to animate His body which is the church.

But Jesus has not left physicality behind. He has taken it with Him into heaven. When the New Testament talks about the church as a body it does so as a metaphor that expresses the diversity of members that make up a unified whole under the headship of Christ (1 Cor. 12). It does not mean the church is a replacement for Christ's physical body. Why not? *Christ does not need a replacement body because He is still embodied.*

The church, in this view, replaces Jesus physically as the institution which will bring about the kingdom on earth. The incarnation is seen in isolation as the event that brings the kingdom, and the mission of the church is to continue the incarnation. So we relate to Jesus primarily as our example. A recent book on missional Christology, for example, tells the story of a speaker asking an audience of 600 people with whom they most identify in the story of the healing of Jairus' daughter in Luke 8. We are invited to be shocked that only six people identified with Jesus. But do we really want lots of people with a messiah-complex! The problem is we are being invited to see Jesus as our model before we see Him as our Saviour. We are invited to respond by continuing His work of salvation rather than putting our faith in His finished work.

In this view the kingdom of God consists of the values, the ethics and the good works that Jesus did on earth and which the church now continues in His name. The difference between the 'now' and 'not yet' of the kingdom is seen as the difference between incomplete and complete rule, and our task is to bridge the gap. Gradually the kingdom will grow in history through the good works of Christians. Fulfilling all the messianic hopes of the Old Testament becomes the task of the church. Jesus gave us a great start, but now the task of completing the job rests on us. What a burden! It is a form of works-righteousness. We may not be working for our personal salvation, but we are working for the salvation of the world through the establishment of God's kingdom on earth.

But the message of the ascension as it is presented in the New Testament is this: Jesus has already established His kingdom. All authority has already been given to Him. In the book of Acts the kingdom is something which is proclaimed and which can be entered. This is what you discover when you look at how Luke uses the term (Acts 1:3; 8:12; 14:22; 19:8; 20:25; 28:23, 31). It is never something that is said to grow or increase. How can it increase when Christ has already been given '*all* authority in heaven and on earth' (Matt. 28:18)? From where could the growth come if Jesus already has all authority? God has placed Him 'far above all rule and authority, power and dominion, and every name that is invoked, not only in the present age but also in the one to come.' (Eph. 1:21) Notice that Paul says in this present age as well as the age to come. Jesus ruling above all is already a reality. This is how things are 'in this present age'. What 'spreads' or 'grows' in the mission of the church is 'the word of God' and 'the number of disciples' (Acts 2:47; 6:7; 9:31; 12:24; 16:5; 19:20).

The growth of the kingdom is a growth in the extent to which it is populated. What grows is the number of people who gladly acknowledge the rule of Christ and so experience that rule as a rule of blessing and freedom. But the 'reality' of Christ's authority does not increase. It is not that Jesus becomes more kingly or that His reign more real through my missionary or social efforts.

There is a further danger with seeing the incarnation as our model for mission in isolation from the cross, resurrection and ascension of Jesus. We can then think our primary role is to identify with the world just as Jesus identified with humanity. The logic of this then becomes the more we identify with the world, the better we are doing our mission.

In fact we call people to an uneasy relationship with their culture. Andrew Walls refers to the indigenising principle of the gospel which means people follow Christ in culture-specific ways. But he also talks of the pilgrim principle which means we no longer belong – we are aliens within what was once familiar. Jesus entered a culture, but also challenged that culture and was rejected by His own.[23] The ascension provides a framework that holds together these indigenising and pilgrim principles because of the bodily ascension of Jesus. Because the One who gives us our identity is absent, the ascension prevents the church being absorbed into the world by absorbing the culture of the world. But because He ascended as a real physical person from a particular time and place He brings human culture into the presence of the Father so that through His humanity He makes a place for all tribes, tongues, nations and cultures to be represented before the throne through Him.

By telling and retelling the story of the ascension we are reminded that the One who gives us our identity is absent. We are not of this world because He is not in this world.

The ascension is the vindication of Jesus and His claims. At His trial before the Jewish council as told in Luke's

---

23 Andrew F. Walls, *The Missionary Movement in Christian History: Studies in the Transmission of Faith*, (Orbis, 1996)

gospel, Jesus is asked whether He is the Christ, God's promised king. He replies: 'If I tell you, you will not believe me, and if I asked you, you would not answer. But from now on, the Son of Man will be seated at the right hand of the mighty God.' They all asked, 'Are you then the Son of God?' He replied, 'You say that I am' (Luke 22:66-71). Jesus is alluding to Daniel 7 and His ascension. The verdict of humanity against Jesus is 'blasphemy' (22:71). Humanity rejects the claim of Jesus to be the king of the world and Son of God. Instead we condemn Him. We all do this as we refuse to live our lives under His lordship. We reject His claims and so we reject His rule. The verdict of the Jewish leaders was not an unusually bad day in the history of humanity. It was a typical day. The only difference was they had the Son of God standing before them, seemingly at their mercy. This is where our rebellion ends, with the condemnation of God's Son.

But, just as Jesus predicted, the verdict of humanity is overturned through the ascension by the heavenly court of appeal. The heavenly scene which Jesus enters on the clouds is a courtroom scene. 'The court was seated and the books were opened,' we are told in Daniel 7:10. Humanity rejected the claims of Jesus and condemned Him to death. Now the heavenly court strips the kingdoms of earth of their power and gives that power forever to Jesus. Jesus is vindicated.

This vindication continues through the work of the Spirit. Jesus links the work of the Spirit to His ascension in John 16:8-11: 'When [the Counsellor] comes, he will prove the world to be in the wrong about sin and righteousness and judgment: about sin, because people do not believe in me; about righteousness, because I am going to the Father, where you can see me no longer; and about judgment, because the prince of this world now stands condemned.' The world judges Christ (through the sin of unbelief), but God overturns that judgment by declaring Christ to be in the right or righteous (through the ascension) and in so doing judges this world and its ruler. The ascension is therefore the vindication of Christ and therefore also the condemnation of the world. The Greek word John uses to describes the Spirit's role can mean both convince and convict (in a manner akin to our English words 'convict' and 'conviction' or 'prove' and 'reprove') and John seems to play on this double meaning. The Father's reversal of the world's judgment leads to our judgment or conviction.

So the ascension reminds us that the world stands condemned. It is condemned by its judgment against Jesus, which has been overturned by God through the ascension of Jesus in triumphant vindication. So, while we love and serve the world, there is a limit to the extent to which we can identify with a world that 'now stands condemned'. Instead, in the power of the Spirit we proclaim Jesus as Lord and call people to repentance. 'The Spirit's office … is not an office of final judgment, or condemnation, but is set in a missiological context … The world, in being "convicted" of that judgment, is not judged finally, but has an opportunity to be the rebellious world no longer.'[24]

---

24   Oliver O'Donovan, *Resurrection and Moral Order*, (IVP, 1986), pp. 105-6.

Conclusion
Who May Ascend?

The Garden of Eden was built on a mountain according to Ezekiel 28:13-14: 'You were in Eden, the garden of God … You were on the holy mount of God.' Eden is portrayed in the Bible as a temple, a place where God and humanity meet, as Greg Beale has shown.[1] But God's intention was that Eden would spread so the whole earth would become a sanctuary in which humanity and God could live together. Yet humanity rejected life with God and as a result we descended from the mountain garden.

---

1   G. K. Beale, *The Temple and the Church's Mission: A Biblical Theology of the Dwelling Place of God*, (Apollos, 2004), and Gregory K. Beale, 'Eden, the Temple and the Church's Mission in the New Creation', in *Journal of the Evangelical Theological Society*, 48:1 (March 2005), pp. 5–31.

At Mount Sinai God began the reconstruction of a meeting place for God and humanity. Moses again ascends a mountain to be shown the heavenly sanctuary, the pattern for its earthly counterpart. But Mount Sinai is a place of fear for the people and it cannot be approached without a mediator: 'When the people saw the thunder and lightning and heard the trumpet and saw the mountain in smoke, they trembled with fear. They stayed at a distance and said to Moses, "Speak to us yourself and we will listen. But do not have God speak to us or we will die"' (Exod. 20:18-19). So Moses ascends to meet God on behalf of the people. But when he descends again he does so to the sound of revelry, to the people of Israel worshipping a golden calf. In the absence of God and His mediator, the people have made a god for themselves.

With the construction of the temple on Mount Zion in Jerusalem, God and His people once again have a mountain meeting place. Psalms 120–134 are 'songs of ascents', sung as pilgrims travelled to ascend Mount Zion to meet with God. Remember God's intention was that the temple-garden of Eden would extend so the whole earth became a temple in which humanity and God dwelt together. Jerusalem is a picture of this (Isa. 4:5-6; Jer. 3:16-17). It is not just in the temple, but in the city as a whole that God resides with His people:

> Great is the Lord, and most worthy of praise,
>   in the city of our God, his holy mountain.
> Beautiful in its loftiness,
>   the joy of the whole earth.
> Like the utmost heights of Zaphon is Mount Zion,
> the city of the Great King.
> God is in her citadels;
>   he has shown himself to be her fortress. (Ps. 48:1-3)

But again God's people are unfaithful and the prophet Ezekiel sees God's glory leaving the temple (Ezek. 10). As a result, Mount Zion is defeated, the temple is destroyed and the people are exiled to the flatlands of Babylon. Ascent has become descent again. Ezekiel, however, is given a vision of a new temple built in a new Jerusalem (Ezek. 40–48) where God's glory will again be among His people (Ezek. 43) and from which will flow a life-giving river (Ezek. 47).

This story of biblical ascent reaches a double climax in Jesus. First, Jesus ascends the hill of Calvary. 'Zion becomes the ironic mountain of death with its man-made trees.'[2] In his Gospel, John describes the cross as an ascent, a lifting up, an exaltation. '"And I, when I am lifted up from the earth, will draw all people to myself." He said this to show the kind of death he was going to die' (John 12:32-33; see also John 3:14-15). 'The raising up of Christ begins, paradoxically, with his crucifixion, and his ascension begins, paradoxically, with his lifting up on the Cross.'[3] Jesus does not ascend *to* the meeting place of God and humanity. He ascends to *be* the meeting place of God and humanity. As He dies the curtain of the temple is torn in two from top to bottom, a sign that we can now come before God (Mark 15:38). Jesus is the temple (John 2:19-22).

Second, Jesus ascends into heaven. The unity between God and humanity achieved at the cross is realised in heaven. There is a man in the presence of God. Human flesh is now with God. And He is there on our behalf. So

---

2   Farrow, *Ascension and Ecclesia*, p. 28.

3   T. F. Torrance, *Space, Time and Resurrection*, p. 110.

much so that Paul can say that we are there with Him. 'God raised us up with Christ and seated us with him in the heavenly realms in Christ Jesus' (Eph. 2:6). We have risen and ascended with God to heaven. The key is that by faith we are united with Christ. As a result, what is true of Him is true of us. His death is our death – we no longer face the judgment of God. His life is our life – we will rise to eternal life after our physical death. And His ascension is our ascension – His presence in heaven is a guarantee of our present access to the Father in prayer and our future presence with the Father in eternity.

'Who may ascend the mountain of the Lord? Who may stand in his holy place?' asks Psalm 24. The answer is: 'The one who has clean hands and a pure heart, who does not trust in an idol or swear by a false god' (Ps. 24:3-4). But where can we find such a person? Those criteria rule out you and me. But the psalm goes on: 'Lift up your heads, you gates; be lifted up, you ancient doors, that the King of glory may come in. Who is this King of glory? The Lord strong and mighty, the Lord mighty in battle' (24:7-8). The Psalmist calls on the gates of Mount Zion to swing open because someone is coming who can ascend the hill of the Lord – the King of glory. This is the king of God's people, the human son of David. But it is also God Himself, the Lord Almighty. This is Jesus, the God-man, the King of glory and the Lord Almighty. He may ascend the hill of the Lord. He may stand before God in the holy place. For He has clean hands and a pure heart. And if you have faith in Christ then you are in Him. His purities, His achievements, His privileges are yours. In Christ *you* have clean hands and a pure heart and so in Christ *you* may ascend the hill of the Lord.

The story ends with John's wonderful vision of ... Well, what is it that John sees? In Revelation 21 he sees a new earth in verse 1, a new city in verse 2 and a new temple in verse 3 ('God's dwelling place'). The chapter introduces us to a new heavens and a new earth, but what John describes is a garden-city. Moreover, a number of the dimensions and features of the city are drawn from Ezekiel 40–48, which describes the dimensions and features of a future temple. And like the Holy of Holies in Solomon's temple, the city that John sees is a perfect cube (1 Kings 6:20; Rev. 21:16-17).

So which is it? Is it a new earth like a city? Or a city like a temple? Or a temple like a city? Greg Beale's argument is that all along it has been God's intention to bring temple, city and earth together. Eden was a temple-garden that God intended would extend throughout the whole earth. Jerusalem was a partial fulfilment of this. The new creation is the ultimate realisation of this: the whole earth is God's city is God's temple. An angel, says John, 'carried me away in the Spirit to a mountain great and high, and showed me the Holy City, Jerusalem, coming down out of heaven from God' (Rev. 21:10). But the bejewelled city that John describes echoes Ezekiel's vision of a new temple which itself echoes the Jerusalem temple which itself echoes Eden (Rev. 21:10-27). Here for the final time God's people ascend 'a mountain great and high' to dwell in the presence of God forever. And from the throne of the Lamb flows a life-giving river that brings healing to the nations (Rev. 22:1-5).

'Who may ascend the mountain of the LORD?' the Psalmist had asked before answering, 'The one has clean hands and a pure heart' (Ps. 24:3-4). And John echoes that answer when he says: 'Nothing impure will ever enter it, nor will anyone who does what is shameful or deceitful, but only those whose names are written in the Lamb's book of life.' (Rev. 21:27) We may not have clean hands and a pure heart, but Christ our King does. And those who by faith are in Christ share His merits. Our names are written in His Book of life. We can ascend the holy mountain to enjoy the presence of God forever. We will ascend. And we have ascended. 'God raised us up with Christ and seated us with him in the heavenly realms in Christ Jesus'(Eph. 2:6). Christ's ascension is our ascension.

An Ascension Hymn

This hymn was written to express something of the glorious significance of the ascension outlined in this book. Its metre is 7777D. We recommend it is sung to the Red Mountain Music tune for the Charles Wesley hymn 'Depth of Mercy'. Sheet music for this tune can be found here:

http://www.redmountainchurch.org/rmm/alb/rmmsheetmusic/DepthofMercy_sheet.pdf

1. *Jesus Christ, ascended priest,*
   passing through the clouds for me,
   entering the Holy Place,
   there to be my surety.
   Interceding in my name,
   he is my security.
   Through His blood, shed once for all,
   I am cleansed eternally.

2. *Jesus Christ, ascended king,*
   comes with clouds to heaven's throne.
   Son of Man with glory crowned,
   rule belongs to Him alone.
   Jesus now empowers His church,
   Jesus now protects His own.
   He is with us to the end
   as we make His gospel known.

3. *Jesus Christ, ascended man,*
   passing through the clouds for me,
   there before the Father's throne,
   our redeemed humanity.
   Human flesh is now with God,
   Jesus is our guarantee.
   He will soon make all things new,
   reign in love eternally.

Tim Chester © 2012.

The Porterbrook Network in partnership with Wales Evangelical School of theology (WEST) provides theological training for new believers through to church leaders, planters and PhD Level. The WESTPorterbrook Network connects the best of the academy to local church and church-planting contexts to deliver gospel-centred training that is biblical, missional, practical, flexible, affordable, accessible and comprehensive at its core. It offers distance learning and residential training courses through its network of learning sites and campuses. In particular the network offers

Porterbrook Learning: a course designed for all Christians to learn how to live gospel-centred lives on mission to their local context.

Porterbrook Seminary: an affordable and flexible college level course for church leaders and planters to train in the context of ministry, with the opportunity of progressing to masters and PhD training through WEST.

The WESTPorterbrook network has grown to host learning sites throughout the UK, the US, Canada, Italy, India, South Africa and Denmark. The materials for Porterbrook learning have also been translated into several foreign languages with more sites and translation in the pipeline.

Christian Focus Publications

Our mission statement –

STAYING FAITHFUL
In dependence upon God we seek to impact the world through literature faithful to His infallible Word, the Bible. Our aim is to ensure that the Lord Jesus Christ is presented as the only hope to obtain forgiveness of sin, live a useful life and look forward to heaven with Him.

Our Books are published in four imprints:

CHRISTIAN
FOCUS

Popular works including biographies, commentaries, basic doctrine and Christian living.

CHRISTIAN
HERITAGE

Books representing some of the best material from the rich heritage of the church.

MENTOR

Books written at a level suitable for Bible College and seminary students, pastors, and other serious readers. The imprint includes commentaries, doctrinal studies, examination of current issues and church history.

CF4•K

Children's books for quality Bible teaching and for all age groups: Sunday school curriculum, puzzle and activity books; personal and family devotional titles, biographies and inspirational stories – Because you are never too young to know Jesus!

Christian Focus Publications Ltd,
Geanies House, Fearn, Ross-shire,
IV20 1TW, Scotland, United Kingdom.
www.christianfocus.com